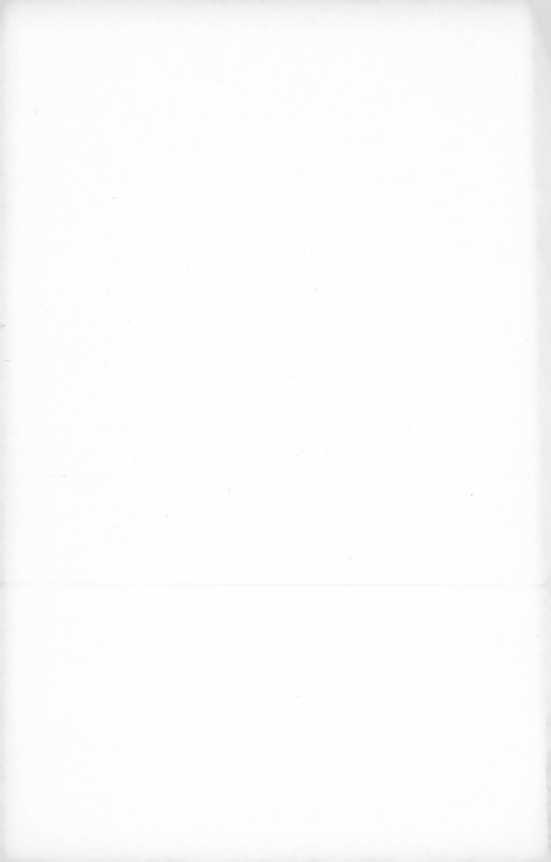

the wyclyf tradition

the
wyclyf
tradition

by
vaclav mudroch

Edited by
Albert Compton Reeves

Ohio University Press . *Athens, Ohio*

Library of Congress Cataloging in Publication Data

Mudroch, Vaclav.
    The Wyclyf tradition.

    Bibliography: p.
    Includes index.
    1. Wycliffe, John, d. 1384. I. Reeves, Albert
Compton. II. Title.
BX4905.M82   270.5'092'4   77-92253
ISBN 0-8214-0403-2

CONTENTS

Foreword

This book began as a doctoral dissertation carried out under the direction of Professor Bertie Wilkinson and submitted to the University of Toronto in 1960, and it is now being published as a contribution to Wyclyf scholarship. Mudroch was primarily concerned with the lively topic of Wyclyf historiography, for as Mudroch wrote of Wyclyf in "Medieval Heresy: Gleanings and Reflections":

> A philosopher pure and simple at first, a royal servant, a religious and political reformer and theoretician, a dogmatic controversialist, an anti-papal writer, a biblical enthusiast—all these personalities he carried in his breast. Who can wonder that modern scholars have been looking for the true Wyclyf for decades and that he is still evading them?[1]

There is an aspect of the incongruous about Mudroch as a scholar of religious dissent: heretics as a group are morbid and dour, but Mudroch was filled with joy, charity, and humanity. He was born in Prague, Czechoslovakia, on 4 April 1924, where his father was Technical Director of Prague's Industrial Faire. He began his schooling in the French government public school in Prague, then moved on to the English government high school and Czech business academy. In 1944–5, during the German occupation, he was engaged in forced labor in a plane factory. Following his secondary education, and after passing special examinations in Latin, Vaclav became a law student at Charles University in Prague, from which he graduated with a doctorate in law in 1949. He married in the same year. He was unable to practice law because of the political situation, and so found manual labor jobs in forestry, stone quarrying, and such.

With his wife, Mudroch left Czechoslovakia illegally for West Germany in 1950. There he worked as a prosecutor for the American occupation forces in Stuttgart, and obtained papers for emigration to Canada. The Mudrochs arrived in 1951 in Vancouver, where Vaclav did manual labor in the lumber industry until his entry into the University of British Columbia in 1952, where he received his B.A. in 1954. After teaching French at U.B.C. for a year, he was awarded a Woodrow Wilson Fellowship that enabled him to enroll at the University of Toronto and study medieval history. While in Toronto, the Mudrochs became Canadian citizens. He obtained the M.A. in 1957, and began to work toward his doctorate. In 1958, following a research year in England, Mudroch was appointed an Instructor in the History Department at the University of Kansas. He was promoted to Assistant Professor in 1961. Mudroch's teaching career at Kansas was singularly successful. The graduating class of 1962 presented Mudroch the annual HOPE (Honor for the Outstanding Progressive Educator) Award in recognition of his professionalism and the stimulation and assistance he gave to students. As one of his students, this Kansas undergraduate was awed by Mudroch's command of language, inspired by his learning, and captivated by his warmth. He knew fully the distinction between advising and counseling his students, and he was ever the master in his classroom, delivering polished lectures, usually without notes. The twinkle in his eye, that could progress to a jolly grin or booming laughter, he shared without discrimination. The shadow over his Kansas years was the start of the illness that would ultimately take his life.

In the autumn of 1963, Dr. Mudroch returned to Canada as an Associate Professor of History at Carleton University in Ottawa. After two years at Carleton, the Woodrow Wilson Foundation commissioned Mudroch to spend a year teaching at Tugaloo College in Mississippi. He wrote to me in October 1965: ''The students are a pleasant surprise . . . , and the desire of the whole lot to learn is hard to imagine to those who are not part of the campus. It is an experience I shall always treasure.'' Mudroch returned to Ottawa in 1966, but the effects of the multiple sclerosis by which he was afflicted were such that he had to abandon teaching in 1967. He was hospitalized for two years, and died in Ottawa on 24 November 1969.

I knew Vaclav Mudroch as a teacher and a friend, and it was not without qualm that I undertook to edit this manuscript. What student would not hesitate before tracking through an admired professor's research? I was happy to discover that Mudroch was a careful and accurate worker, and the flaws I have found in his dissertation were those small slips of typing and reading copy that are the bane of every author. Mudroch did most of his research in the British Museum (now the British Library), and on a recent visit I was able to review most of his work. Unless indicated, all quotations in the text have been checked with the original source, and for the benefit of readers schooled in modern languages translations have been provided for the longer Latin quotations in the text. A sampling of the footnotes has been checked, and I have confidence in their accuracy. I have also attempted in the footnotes, in square brackets, to indicate within limits where scholarship since 1960 has touched upon subjects covered in the text. Very little has been done with the text as it stands beyond refining certain infelicitous phrases. A major editorial departure from the dissertation itself has come through the decision not to publish Mudroch's series of excurses on the general topics of Wyclyf's early years, Wyclyf and the Oxford colleges, his ecclesiastical preferments, Wyclyf and politics, Wyclyf's attack on the Church, and Wyclyf at Lutterworth. These essays are tangential to the subject of Wyclyf historiography, and many would have required the impossibility of extensive revision to have made them appropriate for publicaion at this time. Therefore, though it may not appear to be such, the conclusion of this book was written as a preface to further remarks. As it stands, the subject matter of this book fills an obvious gap in Wyclyf historiography. Margaret Aston has in recent years dealt with the contribution of Wyclyf to the Reformation era (see the Bibliography and footnotes for references), and several writers, such as Herbert Workman and John Stacey, have surveyed the nineteenth- and twentieth-century contributions to Wyclyf studies, but only James Crompton in an article on the ''myth'' of Wyclyf has called attention to the continuing interest Wyclyf held for writers in the intervening centuries and to the usefulness of such a study as Mudroch undertook.

Mrs. Sonja Mudroch has provided information and cooperation in the publication of her husband's thesis, and she has my sincere gratitude. Thanks are also due to two of Mudroch's former students: Dr. Craig A. Robertson, with whom I have discussed the editing of this work, and Mr. Arly Allen, who brought his enthusiasm and the resources of the Allen Press to the project. It is only to be regretted that we shall have no more than this one book from Professor Mudroch, but even without it his memory would remain bright with those whose lives were touched by his.

Albert Compton Reeves

Note

[1] *Essays on the Reconstruction of Medieval History,* ed. Vaclav Mudroch and G. S. Couse (Montreal and London: McGill University Press, 1974), p. 155.

A Note on Spelling

A name whose spelling appears in various medieval manuscripts in 26 variants (A. B. Emden, *A Biographical Register of the University of Oxford to A.D. 1500* [3 vols.; Oxford: Clarendon Press, 1957–59]) can never be spelled correctly. In 1938 the outstanding Wyclyf scholar S. Harrison Thomson suggested that the by then established spelling "Wyclif," adopted by the Wyclif Society and well-nigh universally accepted, be changed to "Wyclyf." To support his plea, Thomson adduced evidence culled both from manuscripts and narrative material of fourteenth-century provenance. (S. Harrison Thomson, "Wyclif or Wyclyf?," *English Historical Review*, LIII [1938], 675–678.) Although his case did not lack logic, he was not followed immediately by his fellow historians. The form "Wyclif," now and then supported by "Wycliffe," was too deeply rooted in literary works to be set aside. Thomson's thesis was buttressed by additional findings of Joseph H. Dahmus ("Further Evidence for the Spelling 'Wyclyf'," *Speculum,* XVI [1941], 224–225). Dahmus discovered four instances of the spelling "Wyclyf" in the register of William Courtenay, archbishop of Canterbury, and followed S. Harrison Thomson in advocating the change to the latter form of the reformer's name.

During my research in the Public Record Office, I came across Exchequer documents connected with the mission to Bruges (P.R.O. Foreign Accounts, E.364/8, and P.R.O., E.101/316/36) in which the name in question was spelled "Wyclyff." Accepting what can be called the official spelling of the royal commissioner to Bruges, I have decided, with a small modification, to spell the name Wyclyf, as it was suggested by S. Harrison Thomson and Joseph H. Dahmus, and follow the example of a handful of writers. This, of course, does not solve the question of the correct spelling. If Wyclyf really comes from the village of Wycliffe, and should oldest available historical evidence be followed, the name should be spelled Wigeclif or Witclive because these are the oldest forms found in the documents (Eilert Ekwall, *The Concise Oxford Dictionary of English Place-Names* [Oxford: Clarendon Press, 1936] and A. H. Smith, *The Place-Names of the North Riding of Yorkshire* ["English Place-Name Society," Vol. V; Cambridge: University Press, 1928]). Herbert B. Workman was not correct, therefore, when he remarked that the spelling "Wiclif" is German and should be avoided (Herbert B. Workman, *John Wyclif,* 2 vols. [Oxford: Clarendon Press, 1926]). Ekwall and Smith have found examples of the spelling "Wigeclif" and "Witclive" in documents dated *c.* 1050 and 1086 respectively.

V.M.

Preface

In the countries lying to the north of the Mediterranean Sea there were times when the student's ambitious aim "to blaze a trail through pathless tracts of the [Muses'] Pierian realm where no foot has ever trod before"[1] did not seem to embody a vainglorious assertion. Today this same world, much older than in the days of Lucretius, presents a different appearance. History as well as the other branches of humanistic studies has yielded to the researcher the bulk of its treasures. It is no wonder that in our own times happy accidents and scientific inventions are increasingly responsible in historical research for results which in not so remote times were solely achieved by the systematic efforts of the historian's intellect.[2] Originality is becoming a scarce commodity. Fortunately, history works not only with facts but also with interpretations, and there was never a lack of opinions. No better example than the life of John Wyclyf may be found whose history presents so rich, confused and contradictory interpretations.

I have tried to look at John Wyclyf especially from the point of view of the "dull controversialists" of the centuries lying between the end of the Middle Ages and the beginning of the modern world. Thus I have ventured to resurrect authors who for the modern reader are often unknown, even though in the times in which they lived they exercised an influence on the reading public which is not equal to the degree of oblivion into which they have sunk since then. My first brief encounters with the religious literature of the sixteenth and seventeenth centuries, originally stimulated by chance references, have convinced me that not nearly enough attention has been devoted to judgments and evaluations of Wyclyf made during those centuries. Ultimately, the strange variety of opinions which I uncovered—not always easily and step-by-step—led me to the conclusion that such an examination would serve two purposes: it might bring to light views hitherto unknown to historians and also reflect in many ways the transformation of European society after the destruction of medieval religious unity, during the growth of what R. H. Tawney has called *The Acquisitive Society*.

I have attempted to penetrate as far as possible behind the examined texts, and expose their sources. The historians of the past were not invariably of the Father Daniel type, that "historian" who "went to inspect the works in the royal library, spent an hour there, and declared he was perfectly satisfied."[3] Despite the scrupulous intent of many of the writers of the past to search for truth, when we reproach some of them today for failing to find it, we may recognize that they owed allegiance more to their religious beliefs than to historical truth. Many accounts of Wyclyf, originating in times of religious strife, are studded with invective against the Catholic or Protestant religion; but once these cherished recriminations and accusations disappear, we mark the old society on the decline.

In our times the story of John Wyclyf and his rebellion against the medieval *ordo* forms with varying degrees of emphasis an integral part of every modern textbook of medieval history.[4] The uncertainty as to what part Wyclyf played in English political life in the latter years of the fourteenth century, and what his teaching really meant still requires interpretation in learned journals,[5] and anthologies of medieval political and theological lore would be incomplete without his name.[6] And yet the recognition of Wyclyf's historical importance was neither spontaneous nor did it come accompanied, as we shall see, with universal enthusiasm. John Lewis, the vicar of Minster, whose "whiggish and low-church views excited"—at least once—"the hostility of his hearers,"[7] was the first author to approach John Wyclyf with respect for, and thorough knowledge of historical documents. The result of his determination "faithfully to represent things as they really are"—the words are not Ranke's—was the publication in 1720 of the first, and for a long time, the best biography of John Wyclyf. The second edition, which Lewis used to refute some infelicitous judgments of Thomas Hearne and others whose views Hearne shared, followed in three years.[8] A third edition, appearing one hundred years after the first, revised and enlarged from the notes left behind by Lewis, laid the foundations, in a more favorable climate of opinion, to the true development of Wyclyf studies.[9] The nineteenth-century historians, especially those writing in the years preceding and following the five hundredth commemoration of Wyclyf's death in 1884, and with it the closely related foundation of the Wyclif Society,[10] rescued the *Morning Star of the Reformation*[11] from relative obscurity and the hitherto private possession of the clergymen, and established him in history as a reformer worthy of general attention.

This work is devoted to the discussion of literature treating of Wyclyf between the *Saeculum Wicklefianum* and the century of Marx, Darwin, and the historians.[12] There exists a surprisingly large number of unknown commentaries dealing with Wyclyf during this period. It is beyond the physical capacity of a lonely researcher to collect every single word of judgment passed upon Wyclyf, and there were many of them. In view of the enormous mass of available and untouched information I have chosen to concentrate on those authors who obviously were important to their contemporaries.

I am well aware that many resounding names with whom I have argued many a point in silence are forgotten and lie buried in the neglected corners of the graveyards of the centuries. They are, I may say, unjustly forgotten. Their pungent prose reads well, and their opinions still retain value. Having had their destiny and their work in front of my eyes for a sufficient length of time to realize how perishable are the works of the human mind, I am, naturally, reluctant to launch my words on the sea of history with the anticipated "divine intoxication of the first league out from land." I would dissimulate my feelings, however, if I did not confess that the discovery of a few books in the British Museum, still uncut after more than one hundred years, was one of the satisfying features of my research.

Vaclav Mudroch
1960

Notes

[1] Titus Lucretius Carus, *De rerum natura libri sex,* i, 926–7, and iv, 1–2. English translation: *On the Nature of the Universe,* tr. Ronald E. Latham (Harmondsworth: Penguin, 1951), pp. 54, 130.

[2] Beryl Smalley, "John Wyclif's *Postilla super totam bibliam,"* *The Bodleian Library Record,* IV (1952–3), 186–205. The text of the article contains the following information:

p. 187: "The trail began from an erasure in MS Bodl. 716 (S.C. 2630)."

p. 188: "The two last erasures are so deep that the writing on the other side of the leaf shows through. The first springs up under the ultra-violet ray .... Without the ray one can just see the *M.* for "Magistrum" and the final *f.*"

[3] Paul Hazard, *The European Mind,* tr. J. Lewis May (London: Hollis Carter, 1953), p. 33.

⁴ The tradition to include the name of John Wyclyf in a textbook of history is an old one. Already in 1729 Johann Heinrich Zopf in his textbook, of which he claims that it was used extensively in many schools and *gymnasien* in Germany and elsewhere, reserved five pages to him, considerably more than the textbook of medieval history would spend on the same subject today. (It may be noted that Zopf's textbook, *Erläuterte Grundlegung der Universal-Historie* [Halle im Magdeburgischen: Carl Hermann Hemmerde], went in fifty years between 1729 and 1779 through seventeen editions.) I have used the 1779 edition, and the references to Wyclyf may be found on pp. 157–162.

⁵ Interest in Wyclyf is not as sustained and constant as that in Luther or Calvin. We can speak of periods of glory and periods of decline in the Wyclyf studies. They can be easily detected by the number of articles published in the last hundred years in various journals and periodicals.

⁶ Ewart Lewis, ed., *Medieval Political Ideas,* 2 vols. (London: Routledge and Kegan Paul, 1954), I, 126–130.

Harry Emerson Fosdick, ed., *Great Voices of the Reformation* (New York: The Modern Library, 1952), pp. 3–34.

Matthew Spinka, ed., *Advocates of Reform,* "The Library of Christian Classics," Vol. XIV (London: S.C.M. Press, 1953), pp. 19–88.

Ernst Staehelin, ed., *Die Verkündigung des Reiches Gottes in der Kirche Jesu Christi,* 3 vols. (Basel: Reinhardt, 1951–55), III, 440–455, includes excerpts in German translation of *De Mandatis Divinis, De Ecclesia, De Officio Regis, De Potestate Papae, De Christo et Antichristo,* and *Trialogus.*

⁷ Thompson Cooper, "Lewis, John," *Dictionary of National Biography,* XI (1909), 1065.

⁸ John Lewis, *The History of the Life and Sufferings of the Reverend and Learned John Wicliffe, D.D.* (London: Knaplock and Wilkin, 1720). The edition of 1723 appeared textually unchanged but was enlarged by "An Advertisement in Defense of the Said History" and "An Alphabetical Explanation of the Obsolete Words Used in it." The quotation is from the Preface, p. XVI. The work had both beneficent and detrimental effects on the development of the Wyclyf studies. It became immediately so authoritative a factual source for the life of Wyclyf that for more than one hundred years no attempt was made to examine John Lewis's statements. On the other hand this biography, complemented with a nice array of original documents, enabled authors of lesser historical perspicacity but equal devotion to the memory of Wyclyf to present to the public the hero of their minds without the hardship of engaging themselves—in the so-called unhistorical eighteenth century—in original research.

⁹ John Lewis, *The History of the Life and Sufferings of the Reverend and Learned John Wiclif, D.D.* (a new edition, corrected and enlarged by the author; Oxford: Clarendon Press, 1820). While the eighteenth-century editions of John Lewis's work on John Wyclyf were responsible for a long period of respectable, if not obsequious, obeisance to his views, the third edition of the same book was followed by works of Robert Vaughan in 1828 and 1853, Walter Waddington Shirley in 1858 and 1865, and especially Johann Gottfried Lechler in 1858 and 1873, without whom the later development of the Wyclyf studies would be unthinkable.

¹⁰ The foundation of the Wyclif Society in 1882 was reported by *The Times,* 1 April 1882, p. 9 in the following words: "A society is founded to remove from England the disgrace of having till now left buried in manuscript, the most important works of her great, early Reformer, John Wyclif."

The quincentenary of the death of John Wyclyf held on 21 May 1884 was an occasion uniting people of different social levels in a well-harmonized outcry against the Papacy. The Lord Mayor of London said on this day: "It was now 502 years since the works of Wycliffe were condemned, and one feature of this commemoration would be an answer to that condemnation by the issue to the world of those works. (Cheers.)." He also added that it was now possible to look at Wyclyf "with unalloyed pleasure." Lord Shaftesbury, after alluding to the times in which he lived as the Sunset of the Reformation, nevertheless assured his audience that "the England of Wycliffe and Tyndale would never again lapse into subjection to the Pope of Rome," (*The Times,* 22 May 1884, p. 10). The commemoration of Wyclyf's death took place in an atmosphere of enthusiasm. Latin works were to be translated in English, an annual Wyclyf prize was to be established, at least in Oxford, and a statue of Wyclyf, it was resolved, was to be erected on the Thames Embankment (*The Times,* 19 May 1884, p. 8 and 22 May 1884, p. 10). The last item concerning the festive year of 1884, *The Times* noticed on 5 November 1885 on page 10. It said that the Wyclif Quincentenary Commemoration Committee wound up its business with a profit of £17–10–0 which were turned over to the Wyclif Society.

[11] The appellation "The Morning Star of the Reformation," commonly affixed to Wyclyf's name in the nineteenth century when nearly all his biographers were Protestant clergymen, is of obscure origin. In the *Bodleian MS e Musaeo 86* (S.C. 3629) better known as *Fasciculi Zizaniorum,* I have found on folio 127v the following marginal comment written by John Bale in the sixteenth century quoting (incorrectly) Ecclesiasticus, 50, 6–8: "Quasi stella matutina [erat–added] in medio nebule, et quasi luna plena in diebus suis [lucet–omitted], et quasi sol refulgens, [sic ille–omitted] effulsit in templo dei."

This passage from Ecclesiasticus was, undoubtedly, a favorite image of Bale's vocabulary. It is repeated in a very corrupted form, which is more like a variation on a theme, though the central words, "stella matutina" remain, both in his *Illustrium maioris Britanniae scriptorum . . . Summarium* (Ipswich, 1548), f. 154v, and in the *Scriptorum illustrium maioris Brytannie . . . Catalogus* (Basel, 1557), p. 450. (The latter is a revised edition of the former.) John Foxe was just as enamoured of the quotation from Ecclesiasticus as Bale was. It found its way into the first edition of the *Martyrology,* and then in all the subsequent ones. Foxe, contrary to Bale, indicates his source, and quotes the text correctly in translation (*Actes and Monuments* [London: Day, 1563], III, 85). Subsequent users of the above mentioned MS. in Oxford, and the printed books in London and on the Continent, might have expanded the words borrowed from Ecclesiasticus to *stella matutina reformationis* but I was unable to trace this Latin title to any specific source. The English wording was used for the first time, as far as I could ascertain, in Francis Augustus Cox, *The Life of Philip Melancthon,* 2nd ed. rev. (London: Gale, Fenner, 1817), p. 562: "John Wicliffe, the morning star of the Reformation, was born near Richmond in Yorkshire, in the year 1324."

[Margaret Aston has attributed the first use of the description "morning star of the Reformation" to Daniel Neal, *The History of the Puritans or Protestant Non-Conformists* (London, 1732–8): "John Wycliffe's Reformation Reputation," *Past and Present,* No. 30 (1965), p. 29. The notion is very much alive as witnessed by E. Routley, *English Religious Dissent* (London: Cambridge University Press, 1960), p. 19, and W. Mallard, "John Wyclif and the Tradition of Biblical Authority," *Church History,* XXX (1961), 50. The title G. H. W. Parker selected for his survey of the history of the Church from Wyclyf to the Reformation was *The Morning Star* (Exeter: Paternoster Press, 1965): ". . . Wycliffe could be called 'the morning star' in the words of Ecclesiasticus, but without implying that he heralded later developments, certainly not in any unique sense . . ." p. 57, n. 3.]

[12] According to William Cave and Henry Wharton, writing in the seventeenth century, the fourteenth century was "saeculum Wicklefianum." It was followed by the "saeculum reformatum." William Cave, *Scriptorum ecclesiasticorum Historia Literaria,* with Appendix contributed by Henry Wharton and Robert Gerius, Editio novissima (Basel: Johann Rudolf Imhoff, 1741–5). The Appendix is dated 1743.

Chapter

1

The Fifteenth-Century Reaction and the Sixteenth-Century Reformation

All the available sources disclose that the appearance of John Wyclyf in history was a moment presaging "ten thousand future sorrows" for the historian. The ideas which he *jactavit in aera* in fourteenth-century England caused at once a division of minds—best exemplified in the written records by the chronicles of Thomas Walsingham and the Monk of Leicester—which has never been closed since.[1] Soon after Wyclyf's death Bohemia split in two parts under the weight of his doctrines, and the young University of Prague was first turned into a battleground of philosophers to become later the graveyard of scholastic philosophy as a whole. John Hus, the student and later the rector of the university, received the message from England as a revelation. Carried by students who studied at Oxford and spent most of their time, as marginal remarks in the surviving Wyclyf manuscripts unerringly lead us to believe, in the Lollard centers at Braybrooke and Kemerton, the words of Wyclyf became the philosophical *credo* of Hus.[2] In the seventeenth century, Jan Amos Komenský (Comenius) published a letter which purported to show the interest of Wyclyf in the reforming zeal of Hus, *bonus miles Jesu Christi,*[3] but the possible pious fraud could never equal the sincerity of those words in which the Czech finished in 1398 on the day of St. Jerome, whom Hus significantly qualifies as *the Slav,* the transcription of Wyclyf's *De Veris Universalibus.* For the bachelor of theology from the village of Husinec in southern Bohemia Wyclyf was "magister venerabilis, sacre theologie verus et magnus professor."[4] The early admiration of Hus for Wyclyf never diminished. At the time when the persecution against the Wyclyfites in England was reaching its climax Hus preached before the multitudes about Wyclyf in terms which brought about his citation to the archbishop of Prague. The members of the clergy who accused Hus remembered especially that Hus expressed the desire "quod vellem animam meam ibi fore, ubi est anima Wikleff."[5] They furthermore objected to the title "venerable" given by Hus to Wyclyf, and they did not leave unnoticed his remark which told the congregation that Wyclyf would shake up many a head.[6] However, Hus's admiration should not be understood as slavish dependence on the words of Wyclyf. In the answer to the depositions of the witnesses against him in 1414, Hus explained his position in the following words: "Quid-quid enim veritatis dixit Wiklef, recipio, non quia est veritas Wiklef, sed quia est veritas Christi."[7]

Jerome of Prague, the follower of Hus in doctrine and death, professed an admiration for Wyclyf which approached that of Hus in intensity, and surpassed it in the matter of graphic exhibition. During the course of his interrogation at the Council of Constance Jerome did not deny that he had adorned his quarters in Prague with a portrait of Wyclyf; he only refuted the allegation that he had placed a diadem on his head.[8]

The University of Prague, divided into four nations according to its Charter of 1348, was deeply affected by the dissemination of Wyclyf's ideas in its halls. While the Czech nation embraced with some exceptions the realist teaching of Wyclyf, the German nation, upholding the nominalist doctrine together with the Poles, stood behind the views of the Church concerning the unheard-of defence by attacks on the future heresiarch. The hostility of the national bodies caused not only an accelerated broadcast of philosophical tracts and the rise of two irreconcilable blocks of students leading in 1409 to the exodus of the Germans, but also the composition of anti-Wyclyfite songs and derogatory pamphlets. Among them the anti-Wyclyfite mass, faithfully following the liturgical parts but perverting its purpose with unsuitable texts, provided an expressive illustration, especially in the *Credo,* of the queer sense of humor of the Teutonic detractors of Wyclyf in early fifteenth-century Prague.[9]

The forty-five articles condemned as heretical at the eighth session of the Council of Constance in 1415 remained for a long period of time the basis for knowing and judging Wyclyf.[10] At a time when a man's life with all its details did not receive as much attention as it would today, the articles constituted a biography whose accuracy, in an age of faith, nobody dared to question, if we except the heretics. The second injunction of the Council concerning Wyclyf was for the medieval man of no additional importance. To dig out Wyclyf's bones from the graveyard of Lutterworth, to have them burnt, and then have the ashes thrown in the river Swift was the inevitable result of applied canon law.[11] The punishment of a heretic was a legal problem, and it is not surprising that lawyers, such as Franciscus Peña, the commentator of Nicolaus Eymeric's *Directorium Inquisitorum,* were able to discuss this aspect of a heretic's fate in terms of cold legal logic, and unmoved by sentiment.[12] It may be safely assumed the second burial in 1428 passed unnoticed and unaccompanied by emotional upheavals on the part of the inhabitants of Lutterworth. It must be admitted that in 1428 the English scene differed in many ways from Wyclyf's days. Since 1401 England belonged with its statute *De heretico comburendo,* passed to please and reward the English Church and Archbishop Arundel for their help in the critical years of 1399 and 1400, to those states which legally retributed heresy by death.[13] The Lollards among the knightly class were dying out—the 1395 manifesto was truly their swan song— and the hopes of Oldcastle perished ignominiously in the fire that consumed his body.[14]

Around 1420 or 1421 Henry V asked personally Thomas Netter of Walden to refute the opinions of the heterodox Christians pullulating in England since the emergence of Wyclyf. Netter, the intellectual power of early fifteenth-century England, acquitted himself of the imposed task admirably. For centuries his work served as the argument against the Wyclyfite heresies above which there was not one more effective.[15] The book was not meant for English home consumption only. It reflected the fear from the rising strength of the Hussites and the expanding scope of the Hussite rebellion. This is what Netter had on his mind when he wrote in the preface to *Doctrinale fidei ecclesiae catholicae contra Witclevistas & Hussitas*:

> Written with God's help against the new heretics, the Wyclyfites, who have lately filled English churches and today enter all Bohemia: in the roots of the faith which Christ, his apostles, and, after them, the holy fathers and teachers from the beginning believed and taught in their own time, I propose to instruct the believers.[16]

Twenty years later Thomas Gascoigne, who criticized sharply the existing disorders in the Church in England, and was not afraid to put in words the hearsay evidence that "J. de Gawnt mortuus est ex . . . putrefactione membrorum genitalium et corporis sui, causata per frequentationem mulierum," was unable to find the tiniest straw of sympathy for *Wiclyffe nequam vita.*[17] A contemporary of Gascoigne, Reginald Pecock, bishop of Chichester, was condemned of heresy and nearly delivered to the secular arm for appropriate punishment. One reason for this extreme measure, which Pecock was able to escape with a public recantation in the November days of 1457, could be ascribed to his endeavor to clear the Christian fold from surviving Lollard influences. Opposing the opinions of the heirs of Wyclyf, he became himself unconsciously contaminated. But, his innocence in this respect could have been proved at the time by a single sentence from his *Repressor of Over Much Blaming of the Clergy*. There Pecock speaks, discussing the disendowment of the clergy, of "oon clerk (but verili to seie oon heretik,)" and he means Wyclyf.[18]

On the other side of Europe, in Bohemia, particularly before the fateful fratricidal encounter of Lipany in 1434 which terminated the military phase of the Hussite movement, Wyclyf was the source for the definition of the theological doctrine then being worked out above all by the radical wing of the Hussites, the Taborites. The Priest Jan Příbram reported in his apology that many modernists (*moderni*)—in the Middle Ages usually a title of disparagement—considered John Wyclyf as the Fifth Evangelist.[19] At the Council of Basel the Czech plenipotentiaries defended the memory of Wyclyf against the calumnies of the assembled and, as a rule, hostile cardinals, and among them especially Peter Payne, called English, protected by diplomatic immunity from the sanctions of the Church, and by sheer distance from the hands of English justice, remembered his master in words which rankled in the ears of the dignitaries.[20] Approximately at the same time in a hamlet in southern Bohemia, the inexhaustible breeding-ground of Czech nonconformism in the Middle Ages, a disillusioned peasant and a thinker in solitude, Petr Chelčický, was finishing his passionate indictment of the Church and society by preaching the return to God, to the purity of pre-Sylvestran Church, to the reign of love and nonresistance to evil. And it was in the many arguments of *Mistr Protiva* (the Opposed Master), for such is the name Chelčický chose to conceal the identity of Wyclyf, that he found comfort for his soul and confirmation of his Christian views.[21]

After the papacy broke the conciliar movement before it resulted in a republican system within the Church—"this pestilent poison" as it was characterized by the bull *Execrabilis* in 1460[22]—and established again its unquestionable supremacy in Church matters, we do not hear of any defense of Wyclyf any more. The *Chronica Boemorum* of the author of *Execrabilis*, hostile to Wyclyf, venomous towards the Hussites, and very often inaccurate, remained unanswered and unchallenged, and unfortunately widespread.[23] John Capistrano preached to the multitudes without being understood and without much evident success in the heart of Europe, and in England the Lollards were forgotten while the Lancastrians and the Yorkists were soaking the soil with their blood before their unmoved and uninterested audience.[24] The beginnings of witchcraft, and the growing infatuation in all the social classes of the fifteenth-century society with the theme of the *Danse Macabre* which are nowadays recognized as unmistakable symptoms of the fading faith of the Middle Ages, were made an integral part of the common expression of life.[25]

In 1493 Hartmann Schedel, the well-known compiler of the *Libri Cronicarum,* published in Nürnberg, ended his work not with the more customary words of thanksgiving to God, but with a poem whose first line, "Morte nihil melius; vita nil peius iniqua," was followed by the existentialist conclusion that ". . . vita est carcer perennis."[26] Under these circumstances, and in this atmosphere of gloom and deadly equality, the information incorporated in the text that Wyclyf's body was exhumed, that his articles in the number of forty-five were condemned, and that he had followers who took their origin from the insanities of the Valdensians seems to the modern reader as an addition of minor importance.[27]

Trithemius's famous bibliography published in 1494 contained among many other names the first list of those writers who wrote "contra insanos Wicleffitas & Hussitas haereticos."[28] We learn that Stephen Patrington was *disputator acutissimus,* and Thomas Netter of Walden was "vir in divinis scripturis eruditissimus & in philosophia Aristotelica nobiliter doctus,"[29] but for Trithemius Wyclyf did not exist. Trithemius's conventional orthodoxy may be discovered in the inclusion of William Ockham and Richard Fitzralph among the (orthodox) *scriptores ecclesiastici.* Of the archbishop of Armagh Trithemius thought that he was ". . . in declamandis sermonibus ad populum excellentis industriae."[30]

The Englishman Wyclyf had his Italian parallel in Savonarola, who could not escape the wrath of the papacy, the displeasure of Alexander VI, and the volatile character of the southern rabble. Authority was becoming brute force; it could hardly become a reforming force coming as it was from the clergy of Italy, whose orthodoxy had been much altered by Renaissance and pagan ideals of rediscovered antiquity. The Fifth Lateran Council, which kept on sitting inordinately long to achieve disappointingly little, illustrated the apathy of the Christian body, fatigued after protracted struggles, and while having the desire to rule lacked the strength to live. A false feeling of security reigned in the opening years of the sixteenth century in Europe. The conflicts of the past century seemed to be forgotten, feelings which were bruised or battered were healed, time passed, people forgot.

In 1517 Martin Luther nailed his ninety-five theses on the church door in Wittenberg.[31] In 1520 he appeared in Leipzig before ecclesiastical dignitaries to explain, to modify, to retract his views on the Church. Such were the expectations of the Church prelates and Charles V. But, Luther did not disavow his views to become the prisoner of the Council's arguments. He defied the authority of the Church and proudly proclaimed among other assertions that Hus was unjustly condemned at Constance;[32] later, after he had read the works of Hus sent to him from Bohemia, he went on to exclaim: "We are all Hussites without knowing it."[33] His investigator Eck mentioned in Leipzig the name of Wyclyf, but Luther had passed it by as though he had never heard it before.[34] It seemed as if Wyclyf had vanished from the intellectuals's minds. But the protest of Luther brought back to the minds of those who opposed the sovereignty of Rome, its secular character, its avarice, its degenerate way of life. The revival of the name Wyclyf among the Protestants precipitated his revival among the Catholics, and the discussion concerning his deserts generated by the trials of Luther was one of the most acrimonious of the sixteenth century. Owing to the fact that toleration was not yet a part of either creed or way of life, the words and arguments had a force and liveliness which remain unsurpassed in the annals of literature. Those were the times when the verb *to lie* was still a part of the writer's vocabulary.[35]

The invention of the printing press, which Christopher Cellarius (Keller) considered more useful for mankind than the discovery of the New World, increased the circulation of books in the hands of the reading public, which was growing more and more numerous with the penetration of learning from the South and demands of a more complex civilization.[36] At the same time the writing of books for the printing press and not for a limited number of intellectual giants became a part of the intellectual's life. Discussions formerly confined to the university or cathedral church, and conducted in the rarified atmosphere of medieval scholasticism were now on a large scale broadcast into the streets of the towns, channeled into the minds of its inhabitants now guided, if not governed, by secular rulers. For the Church of Rome the sixteenth century was a period of defense conducted both by physical and spiritual arms. The Council of Trent and the foundation of the Jesuit Order were not the only measures adopted to buttress the undermined constitution of the Church. Books published with the episcopal *Imprimatur*, already introduced at the end of the fifteenth century in Cologne and warmly approved by Popes Sixtus IV and Innocent VIII, became part of the canon law in 1564 by the bull *Dominici gregis*, and served the same purpose.[37] The Church's literary defense was a bitter and tenacious polemic against its detractors to vindicate its stand, and to remind the Christian of its uncompromising attitude towards movements of protest in the past. *Mirrors of Heretics* were published in nearly all the Catholic countries with remarkable success though not with unrestrained enthusiasm on the part of the Church, for oblique condemnations of the new medium, which the Church was compelled to adopt to combat its opponents using the same weapon, were not rare. In the sixteenth century Ambrosius Catharinus deplored the fact that "nowadays the Scripture comes into the hands of all. The ignorant, the irreverent, and frail women add opinion on the most difficult questions, even on predestination by God, grace, free will, and other matters over which the brightest minds have labored and gone wrong."[38] Claudius Coussord, writing eight years later in 1548, exclaimed, "O damnabilis sciendi cupiditas," when he spoke of the current practice of translating the Scriptures into the vernacular.[39] In this new literature the name of Wyclyf was not forgotten. The work of Thomas Netter of Walden, which earned the author a letter of gratitude from Pope Martin V, was remembered, and was put into press immediately after the great refusal of Luther in 1520.[40] The defenders of the faith in the sixteenth century were given a weapon which they wielded with great dexterity.

Among the first writers who took up arms against the danger of the Lutheran heresy was the Dominican Inquisitor, Bernardus de Lutzenburgo (Bernard of Luxembourg), with his *Catalogus haereticorum*, first published in 1522.[41] The author devoted the first part of his *Catalogus* to the discussion of principles bearing on heresy, and in the second part he enumerated the outstanding heretics and heresiarchs of the past ages. (Even the blind military leader of the Hussites, John Žižka, was not spared, and found his way into the select company.)[42] Bernard did not abandon the medieval practice of quoting authorities. Bent on stressing the unalterable position of the Church towards the heretics, he construed his principles with words which were not his. Despite the lack of originality his selections left the reader with the clear impression what was meant by heresy. Heretics were beasts: "Canes, . . . lupi rapaces, . . . serpentes, . . . corpiones, aculeos habentes, insuper et dracones squamosi, basilisci infectivi et interfectivi, . . . aspides, . . . porci immundi."[43] He invoked the authorities of Gotfridus de Trano to impress upon his Catholic readers that they can ". . . hereticos propria auctoritate spoliare, quia ecclesia generalem eis auctoritatem prestitit, ut eos exterminent."[44] And for this purpose *gladius materialis* was given to the emperors, which sounded like a gentle reminder to Charles V to do his duty. After the abstract prin-

ciples came the concrete examples. It is here that we meet the name
of Wyclyf under the heading *Wicleffite.* His knowledge of Wyclyf was
spotty, and seriously behind his knowledge of the Hussite rebels. But
then, there was no pope to write the history of England! According to
Bernard, Wyclyf began to teach his foolish things (*insania*) in 1394.[45]
Bernard admits on the authority of Joannes Nider that Wyclyf was of
a keen intellect (*professor, acer ingenio*) but because of his errors and
life not only a heretic but a heresiarch. He mentioned the fact Wyclyf
wrote both in English and Latin, and ended his short notice with the
statement that Wyclyf's articles were *valde occulti.* As an afterthought
Bernard added that Wyclyf's works were brought to Bohemia by Nicolas Faulfiss, thus following Pius II whom he dutifully acknowledged
as his guide. In the fourth edition of 1537 Bernard of Luxembourg
inserted the Lollards among the heretical ranks on the authority of
Netter's *Liber de sacramentalibus,* and added these words: "Et dicti
haeretici fuerunt discipuli impii Iohannis Vuicleff, quos sequitur hodie
Martinus Luterus."[46]

Although most Catholic theologians of the time were slow to recognize the success of early Protestantism, at least one orthodox, Doctor Johann Fabri, attempted in 1528 a comparison, under the Pauline
motto "Todt ist der Buchstab allein der Geist lebendig," of the teachings and books of John Hus and John Wessel with those of Martin
Luther, and discovered that he was unable to omit the name of Wyclyf.
There is in his words sympathy for a Hus who might have erred in-
nocently, but there is only utter contempt for Wyclyf, whose articles,
unfortunately accepted by Hus, were so horrible that no writing could
either hold or suffer them.[47]

From the same polemical field in Germany, where the most deter-
mined effort was made to trace Luther's heretical origin to that of Hus
and Wyclyf, came the first attempt to synchronize the teachings on the
Eucharist of the three who "freulich un nerrisch einer den andern fur
ein heylige helt."[48] Cochlaeus, after discussing in incisive terms the
various points of view, came to the opinion that they had nothing in
common. However he could not refrain from remarking that Hus was
more pious than either Wyclyf or Luther. One may read between the
old lines the author's unexpressed thought: How could Hus have followed Wyclyf?[49]

In France on the eve of the religious wars an author, Caudius Coussord, whose views on the spread of knowledge we have already noted
above, found an affinity—following the tradition established in France
by Chancellor Gerson—between the tenets of the Valdensians and
those of Wyclyf, and maintained with greater certainty than the master

himself that in his doctrine on the Eucharist Wyclyf said that after the words of consecration the bread remained in the host together with the body of Christ, and distinguished this view from the teachings of the Valdensians and Luther.[50]

In 1548 across the Channel in England John Bale, a converted Divine of the Church of England who started his life with the education in a Carmelite monastery and "paid his debt to nature" as prebendary of Canterbury, published a book entitled *Summary of Illustrious Writers of Greater Britain.*[51] In this work Bale tried to keep the names for posterity of those English writers whose works after 1537 the new proprietors of the "superstycyouse mansyons" used to "scoure theyr candelstyckes, and some to rubbe their bootes" before "they solde them to the grossers and sope sellers."[52] The space reserved for Wyclyf does not tire the eyes, and the information presented to the reader does not overwhelm the mind. Today Bale's account is without any value as far as the pure facts are concerned. His poetical facts, and their influence on the formation of a standard picture of Wyclyf among the growing Protestant community, have a long history. It was Bale who decreed that Wyclyf was a tool in the hands of God against the Antichrists. It was Bale who said that Wyclyf was the Elias of his time, the morning star and all the other epithets in Ecclesiasticus 50.6–8. He was the embodiment of David fighting with the lions, the opponent of the wretched *gens monachorum,* the protégé of Edward III who assured his security among *ferocissimos Sodomae tyrannos.*[53] Bale is also responsible for a few mistakes which on account of his established reputation remained unchallenged and uncorrected for centuries, and some are repeated even today. In the 1548 edition he sent Wyclyf to seek exile after the death of Edward III—*ut Annales tradunt*—in Bohemia. He spread information that Wyclyf translated into English the complete Bible, and he did not escape the trap of the false date of 1387 when he mentioned the year of his death.[54] Considering the fact that Bale drew his information from the many notes left behind by Leland, who transcribed the deposition of John Horne to Thomas Gascoigne on the death of Wyclyf, it is difficult to believe that Bale was a careful student of documents.[55] Nevertheless, he was the first to collect and publish the titles of Wyclyf's works. The 154 titles from the first edition, and the 218 of the Basel edition of 1557 were never fully identified and could not therefore be assigned to the Evangelical doctor who was a "most pious man" and belonged by right to any Catalogue of Saints.[56]

In comparison with Bale's brief and unreliable biography of Wyclyf, the account of the martyr by his compatriot, fellow-exile, and in the end vindicated (by the happy turn of events) opponent of the Catholic church, John Foxe, is not even today devoid of historical value. It not only expressed the belated moral indignation of the English public, then for the first time properly tempered, over the treatment reserved to Wyclyf in the two preceding centuries, but served—and the number of editions provides the irrefutable evidence—as the only trustworthy guide to Wyclyf's and other martyrs's lives for the English Protestant for many years to come. The *Actes and Monuments* is a prodigious work bearing witness both to Foxe's ability to compile material damaging the Catholic church, and to his devotion to the Protestant cause.[57] The first English edition of 1563 opens, as all the following ones, with a calendar of martyrs and a mistake of chronology. John Wyclyf's name is commemorated on 2 January, and his death is set on the indestructible year of 1387.[58] In the first pages of the text Foxe introduces his audience to the Christians such as the Valdensians who suffered the true faith in pre-Protestant times, and approaches quite early the appearance of the "valiant champion of the truth" in the Church history of the fourteenth century.[59] There was a need for a valiant champion in those days as, "In stede of Peter and Paul men occupide their time in studying Aquinas and Scotus." Wyclyf was of a different disposition, and Foxe explains the leitmotif for his inclusion in the martyrology in these words:

> Althoughe it be manifest and evident inough, that there were divers and Sondry before Wickliffe's time, whiche have wresteled and laboured in the same cause and quarrel, that our country man Wickleffe hath done: Whom the holy ghost [Bale said: *pater eternus*] hathe from time to time, raised and stirred up in the churche of God, to vanquish and overthrow the great errours which daily did grow and prevayle in the world.

Wyclyf, as in Bale, is the "morning starre, the mone being full in her course, the bright bemes of the sonne." He saw the "fylthy inventions of Bishops" and could not refrain from "bewayling in his mind the general ignorance of the hole world."[60] Foxe inserts into the narrative the first English translation of the Papal bull sent by Gregory XI to, in the opinion of Foxe, Richard II, and is aroused by its text to the following remark: "This example of barbarous crueltie, sprong up or come into the Christen Hierarchy, that they will straight condemn unto death him whom not only they have not overcome with anye argumentes, but also not once admonished for no other cause, but only for that he semeth unto them an hereticke?"[61] The value of the short but passionate defence of Wyclyf is enhanced by the inclusion of seven translated documents—some of them abridged—which undoubtedly spoke to the avid reader with the same eloquent language as did Foxe.[62]

The second edition appeared in 1576, thirteen years after the first one. The part dealing with Wyclyf is expanded, and bears marks that John Foxe did not read the St. Albans Chronicle—that is, Walsingham—in vain.[63] Wyclyf is still the martyr "whom the Lord (with the lyke zeale and power of spirite) raysed up here in England, to detect more fully and amply the poyson of the Popes doctrine, and false Religion set up by the Friers," but John Foxe notes for the first time that in his "opinions and assertions, albeit some blemishes perhaps may be noted."[64] It would not be against the tradition of the Anglican Church to venture the view that Foxe was disturbed, as many Anglican divines were in the following centuries, by Wyclyf's views on dominion, that is property, but it would be unjust to say that Foxe's enthusiasm for Wyclyf suffered a decline. On the other hand, after 1563, more space is used to criticize the times in which he lived than enlarge the description of his life. Foxe mentions that there was a "horrible darkness of ignoraunce," and Wyclyf wished "to revoke and call backe the Church from her Idolatry to some better amendment, especially in the matter of the Sacrament of the body and blood of Christ."[65] Foxe does not discuss the "matter of the Sacrament" or the merits of Wyclyf's attack but takes advantage of the incident to write how "the whole glut of Monkes and beggyng friers were set on a rage or madness, which (even as Hornets with their sharpe stinges) did assayle this good man on every side: fighting (as is sayd) for their aultars, paunches, and bellies."[66] It is not daring to imagine how these Falstaffian words pleased the Protestant in the age of Shakespeare.

The endeavour of Bale and Foxe to justify the ways of Wyclyf in the eyes of the public was not shared in the country which one hundred and fifty years previously had faced the hostile world ready to reform the society with the sword in one hand and the writings of Hus and Wyclyf in the other. After 1526 and the battle of Mohacs, where the idea of the Czech state, we may say with hindsight, had sunk in the slough of despondency from which it never re-emerged, the Habsburgs sat on the throne of the Bohemian kings. In the country were Lutherans, Utraquists, and Czech Brethren, but the royal family was Catholic. This fact did not escape the attention of the legal-minded and powerful office-holders. Johannes Dubravius (Jan Skála z Doubravky a Hradiště), bishop of Olomouc, in his *Historiae regni Boiemiae de rebus memoria dignis* dedicated *Ad inclytissimum Regem Boiemiae Maximilianum* is in 1552 fighting the fight of the Jesuits.[67] Hus, he writes, was insolent but he became unbearable on the day when he stumbled upon Wyclyf and his work *Alythia* (*Trialogus*). Wyclyf was neither a saint nor a professor of theology but a heretic condemned in England. Moreover the title he used for his work was deceptive. It was more correct to say, such is the view of Dubravius, that it "ruinam & interitum omnium in Ecclesia ritum, atque cerimoniarum continet."[68] After several generations the world had changed.

In twenty-five more years Daniel Adam of Veleslavín published *An Historical Calendar,* and the dedication proved to whom it was addressed: "To the Gentlemen Mayors and Aldermen of the City of Prague, to the Gentlemen, Friends and Compatriots Dear to me, and Graciously Inclined."[69] The gentlemen had to be spared from possible mental shocks. The founder of the first Czech dynasty, a peasant according to legend, was no more historically and socially acceptable. Not a peasant, Veleslavín said, but a knight ploughman was Přemysl.[70] After this introduction the content of the *Calendar* is no more a surprise. We read that on the sixth of July the memory of Hus was commemorated in the churches, but when Veleslavín discusses the burning of Wyclyf's books in Prague on 16 July 1410, we have to be satisfied with the statement that there were various opinions concerning the burning. When he comes to 31 December, Veleslavín copies Bale, and in the best traditions of historical objectivity, notes that on that day in 1387 *Mistr Jan Wigleff Engkis* died, and was buried in his church at Lutterworth.[71] In Bohemia in 1590 the bell had tolled the end of a great even though unsuccessful revolution.

In Southern Europe there was one people which was always interested in the heterodox movements of the fifteenth century, and never lacked writers to discuss the origins and the meaning of the Wyclyfite heresy. In the fifteenth century chief among them was Turrecremata.[72] In the sixteenth century the problem was approached by another writer at once more systematic and more violent than the cardinal: Alphonsus à Castro Zamorensis, the *princeps poenalistarum*. The arguments, conclusions, and conjurations of Castro marked the strongest literary opposition of the Church against the heretics after the appearance of Luther. Nothing else in the sixteenth century equals in violence the superb contempt of the Spaniard for violators of Christian unity. Sometimes the contempt was accentuated by the use of cadaverous irony as when he exhorts his readers to have pity on the Wyclyfites because their minds were disturbed (*insaniunt*). Then he adds with the same breath "si insaniunt, iustius esset eos catenis vincere, quam argumentis."[73] Castro linked Hus to Wyclyf and his works ". . . a quibus . . . [Hus] suum venenum hauriebat," and he qualified both as descendants of Arius in view of their belief that priests were the equals of bishops.[74] He explained that the three heretics were driven to this conclusion by the fact that they did not reach the episcopal dignity.[75] The argument, which passed from Thomas Netter of Walden to Polydore Vergil, from both of whom it might have been borrowed by Castro, was strengthened by the authority of St. Augustine, who analyzed, as the writer knew, the Arian view in his book *De Heresi.* The work of Castro, divided in topics consisting of articles of faith questioned by heretics of all ages, is the most systematic treatise on heresies of immediate post-Lutheran times. Wyclyf or Wyclyfites, whom he separated from the Lollards because "hoc est haereticis peculiare, ut nesciant tenere unitatem,"[76] are mentioned in connection with baptism, benediction, church chant, confession, confirmation, tithes, church, bishop, future contingency, canonical hours, indulgence, labor, monasticism (*monachatus*), sin, purgatory, priesthood, relics, *studia generalia,* saints, and extreme unction.[77] The outburst against Wyclyf, however, reached its climax under the topic *subditus* (spurious), which Castro approached after he had cleared the way for the full Church recognition of the sanctity of property in the discussion under the topic *paupertas.*[78] Castro, who thought that Wyclyf flourished around 1380,[79] assailed Wyclyf in the following terms:

> There is no aspect of the condition of the Church not stung by John Wyclyf, none of its powers undisparaged. He is not himself content to deny obedience and submission to his own superiors, even persuading his subordinates to do the same. And not thinking this to be enough, he must make the subordinate superior to those set over him and vassals superior to their lords. Such a man is Wyclyf, who in order to acquire the support of the people, has fallen into this insane and deadly error, than which none other could be more ruinous . . . . O so pitiable would be a state which would be governed according to Wyclyf's dictates. For in such a state all coarse men, unlearned, wicked, plunderers, adulterers, and liars wish to rule their lords and masters, and, what would be worse, they would violently attack their lords and superiors, and yet be punished by no one, but persist in their villainy unscathed. For then would all things truly be confounded. Youth would revolt against age, the worthless would rise up against the noble, foolish against the wise, student against master, and children against parents. For this government would be a sink hole, or (shall I be more blunt) an unspeakable abyss. What would a people not do who have been given such license? For the people would be like a wild and ferocious beast, and more wild and savage than any other.[80]

Castro's work did not stop the controversy centered around the dead Wyclyf. In 1565 there appeared in Lyon what may be called the first attempt at a biography of Wyclyf, a tract entitled *La Vie de M. Jean Wicleff.*[81] It is not the originality of Crespin, who worked with Foxe's *Actes and Monuments* within his reach, which attracts the historian's attention but rather the colorful application of the French language. The suggestive clarity of Crespin's prose is clearly designed to demonstrate that in the fourteenth century Wyclyf was "une seule bien petite estincelle de la pure doctrine."[82] His life, which the writer described in proper relief from 1372, was traced from the small beginnings of the dispute with Cunningham to the bulls of Pope Gregory XI, *ce diable de pape,* aiming at condemnation of Wyclyf in England.[83] In the eyes of the Frenchman these bulls "ne contiennent autre chose que menaces plus que barbares, violences tyranniques, & ie ne say quelles paroles orgueilliuses, plus seantes à la gueule d'un diable, qu'à la bouche d'un homme."[84] Crespin accepted 1387 as the death of Wyclyf and ended his temperamental defense with a sigh which since then has been echoed many more times: "Il seroit à desirer que ses livres nous fussent demeurez."[85] He consoled himself, however, with the fact that certain have been preserved "pour monstrer que Dieu a tousiours eu des serviteurs fideles, qui ont resisté aux erreurs du monde."

In the same decade in which the French Protestant public was offered an apology for John Wyclyf written by a Frenchman, Cologne was the scene of publication of the *dernier cri* in the production of the mirrors of heretics. *De Vitis, Sectis, et Dogmatibus omnium Haereticorum* by the Frenchman Gabriel Prateolus Marcossius was, as the author admitted in the usual elaborate title, a compilation.[86] The writers he indicated as his main authorities were, to give a slight idea whom we do not recognize as such any more, Claudius Espencaeus, Claudius Sanetesius, Franciscus Horantius, Fredericus Staphylus and Georgius Vuicelius.[87] Prateolus accepted the already current view that Wyclyf was "ingenio quidem valde acri, & eloquentia non mediocri," and thought that he flourished about the year 1352 in the time of Emperor Charles IV and Pope Clement VI.[88] More interesting is the relationship he found between Wyclyf and Archbishop Fitzralph of Armagh. According to Prateolus Wyclyf's teaching concerning the power of the priest and his equal powers with those of the bishop in his absence was derived from the works of *Armacanus.* The reader is not left in doubt as to what was thought of such a doctrine in some Catholic circles in the sixteenth century. In the margin the note says: *Armacani haeresis.*[89]

Before he died Prateolus published a book in Paris under his French name and analyzed the state and success of the Church in the form of a general and universal chronicle.[90] Wyclyf was again on its pages. This time he flourished in 1363. The forty-five condemned articles were reproduced, and the dry collection of inaccurate facts in the previous composition was exchanged for psychological *aperçus.* It was now

Wyclyf's pride and overconfidence in the subtlety of his own mind (a common attribute of all the heretics) which led him to attempt the subversion of the Christian republic. Therefore he was not only a heretic but also a heresiarch.[91] The reasons for the heresy of Wyclyf were indicated but by no means connected with it. Du Préau, however, was sincere enough to admit that the Church was badly governed at the time of Wyclyf and that the kings did not know how to reign. Richard II was not only a *fainéant,* but also a man of effeminate manners and completely entranced by the charms of his wife. Moreover, he was more concerned with designing clothes for his wife than correcting his faults and following his royal rights.[92] In addition, Du Préau seems to imply, everything was possible in England: Was not her people rash and inconstant by its very nature?[93]

France was not the only French-speaking country in Europe that was interested in Wyclyf. Sixteenth-century Geneva was a religious center in Europe which, under the leadership of Calvin, brought together all those who were dissatisfied with the unfinished revolution of Luther and the humanists around him, and attempted with energy, under the guidance of Calvin's logical mind, to make from the Scriptures an irreducible religious geometry. Théodore de Bèze was the right hand of Calvin and the politician and the historian of the Geneva movement. In 1580 he wrote a book in Latin which, as the title indicated, was designed to present to the public the true portraits of all those illustrious men in piety and doctrine of whose work God availed himself to re-install true religion in the various countries of Christendom.[94] The success of the publication led to its translation into French by Simon Goulart in the following year. It is here that we find, in the changed conditions reigning in Europe after the Peace of Augsburg and the enunciation of the principle *cuius regio eius religio,* the following *vrai pourtrait* of Wyclyf: "L'Angleterre a dequoy se glorifier à iamais (encores que depuis elle ait souillé ceste gloire) de ce qu'elle a produit Iean Wiclef, le premier, en la fin de tant d'annees, qui a osé denoncer la guerre à la paillarde Romaine, laquelle se mocquoit si audacieusement des Rois de l'Europe enyvrés de sa boisson."[95] Bèze, oblivious of the Gregorian theme of one *respublica christiana,* so deeply rooted in the medieval world from which he barely stepped out, rejoiced that the wound inflicted by the sword of God's word brandished by Wyclyf did not heal, and remained incurable. He also started a tradition which was to be revived later, and led, especially in the nineteenth century, to disastrous esthetic effects: he composed a poem on Wyclyf. Bèze made it clear to his audience that Wyclyf was endowed with superhuman courage; he was the deliverer of Europe from a cruel bondage and the flames that burned his bones were licking Antichrist himself.[96] The poem, as even cursory reading reveals, is more remarkable for indicating the prevailing atmosphere in Geneva than for its artistic merits.

In the same year in which Bèze was adoring Wyclyf in prose and poetry, Sebastian Medicis, a papal protonotary, published a work in Florence which purported to be the *Summa omnium haeresum et Catalogus schismaticorum, haereticorum et idolatrarum.*[97] The author followed the steps of Castro. He enlarged the scope of the book with the addition of new topics also where Wyclyf was concerned, but he had nothing to say for the historian which was not said before in the same century. In addition, the unrestrained and vigorous language of Castro gave way to a mellifluous tongue of a more diplomatic but less interesting *Medicis*. The publication is evidence that heresy was a favorite subject of the reading public, and the desire to know is often accompanied by the readiness to doubt. At the end of the sixteenth century the Church was still fighting a rear-guard action.

In some countries even rear-guard action was no longer possible. Thus, Robert Abbot, a "minister of the Word of God in the Citie of Worcester," could write, faintly echoing the arguments of Wyclyf while refuting the views of a "secret cavilling Papist": "What a grosse and swinish imagination is this, that by a corporall entrance of Christes bodie into ours, we must be made one with Christ, as man and woman by corporall coniunction become fleshe?"[98]

Notes

[1] The first entry in Thomas Walsingham's *Historia Anglicana* concerning Wyclyf contains the following words: "Per idem tempus surrexit in Universitate Oxoniensi quidam Borealis, dictus 'Magister Johannes Wyclef', saecularis [in] Theologia, tenens publice in scholis ac alibi Conclusiones erroneas et haereticas, ac statui universalis Ecclesiae contrarias, et absurdas; et praecipue contra monachos et alios religiosos possessionatos venenose sonantes." In the course of the narrative Wyclyf becomes: "Antichristi discipulus," "versipellis Johannes Wyclyff," "vetus hypocrita, angelus Sathanae, Antichristi praeambulus, non nominandus Johannes Wicliffe, vel potius Wykbeleve, haereticus," "Collega Sathanae." Recording Wyclyf's death, Walsingham adds the following epithets to his name: ". . . organum diabolicum, hostis Ecclesiae, confusio vulgi, haereticorum idolum, hypocritarum speculum, schismatis incentor, odii seminator, mendacii fabricator." Thomas Walsingham, *Historia Anglicana,* ed. H. T. Riley, 2 vols. (London: "Rolls Series," 1863–4), I, 324, 345, 450, 451; II, 119. The Monk of Leicester introduces Wyclyf in the following way: "In istis temporibus floruit magister Johannes Wyclyfe rector ecclesiae de Lutturworthe in comitatu Leycestriae, doctor in theologia eminentissimus in diebus illis. In philosophia nulli reputabatur secundus, in scholasticis disciplinis incomparabilis." The appreciation of Wyclyf as a scholar is re-emphasized in the *Chronicle* at exactly the same time as his followers are blamed for sowing discord among the English people: "Nam sicut magister eorum Wyclyf potens erat et validus in disputationibus super caeteros, et in argumentis nulli credebatur se-

cundus . . . ." Knighton, incidentally, is much more severe to Wyclyf's followers than he is to Wyclyf. In *Chronicon Henrici Knighton vel Cnitthon Monachi Leycestrensis,* ed. Joseph Rawson Lumby, 2 vols. (London: "Rolls Series", 1895), II, 151, 187.

[2] John Wyclif, *Tractatus de Ecclesia,* ed. Johann Loserth (London: "Wyclif Society", 1886), p. 47. John Wyclif, *De Dominio Divino Libri Tres,* ed. R. L. Poole (London: "Wyclif Society", 1890), p. 249.

[Mudroch was speaking broadly in this sentence; Hus was not merely a Bohemian Wyclyfite. For a succinct comparison of the two, see G. Leff, "Wyclif and Hus: A Doctrinal Comparison," *Bulletin of the John Rylands Library,* L (1967–8), 387–410. Wyclyf's early impact outside of England continues to attract scholarly attention. Note the recent contributions of Miroslav Brandt, "Wyclifitism in Dalmatia in 1383," *Slavonic and East European Review,* XXXVI (1957–8), 58–68; Anne Hudson, "A Lollard Compilation and the Dissemination of Wycliffite Thought," *Journal of Theological Studies,* N.S., XXIII (1972), 65–81; *idem,* "A Lollard Compilation in England and Bohemia," *ibid.,* N.S., XXV (1974), 129–40; Vaclav Mudroch, "John Wyclyf and Richard Flemyng, Bishop of Lincoln: Gleanings from German Sources," *Bulletin of the Institute of Historical Research,* XXXVII (1964), 239–45; Margaret Schlauch, "A Polish Vernacular Eulogy of Wycliff," *Journal of Ecclesiastical History,* VIII (1957), 53–73; František Šmahel, "*Doctor evangelicus super omnes evangelistas*: Wyclif's Fortune in Hussite Bohemia," *Bulletin of the Institute of Historial Research,* XLIII (1970), 16–34; and H. M. Swiderska, "A Polish Follower of Wyclif in the Fifteenth Century," *University of Birmingham Historical Journal,* VI (1957–8), 88–92. For links between Wyclyf and Hus, see G. A. Benrath, "Wyclif und Hus," *Zeitschrift für Theologie und Kirche,* LXII (1965), 196–216; B. A. Vermaseren, "Nieuwe Studies Over Wyclif en Huss," *Tijdschrift voor geschiedenis,* LXXVI (1963), 190–212; and Michael Wilks, "*Reformatio Regni*: Wyclif and Hus as Leaders of Religious Protest Movements," *Studies in Church History,* IX (1972), 109–30.]

[3] Jan Amos Komensky, *Historia fratrum bohemorum* . . . (Halae: Typis et impensis Orphanostrophii, 1702), p. 10.

The letter was written in 1410 by Richard Wyche, a follower of Wyclyf. The answer of Hus is printed in F. Palacký, ed., *Documenta Mag. Johannis Hus* (Prague: Tempsky, 1869), pp. 12–14.

See also R. L. Poole, "On the Intercourse between English and Bohemian Wycliffites in the Early Years of the Fifteenth Century," *English Historical Review,* VII (1892), 306–311. Recent discussions on the migration of ideas from England to Bohemia are to be found in the following works: Otakar Odložilik, *Wyclif and Bohemia, Two Essays* (Prague: Published by the author, 1937), *passim;* R. R. Betts, "English and Čech Influences on the Husite Movement," *Transactions of the Royal Historical Society,* 4th series, XXI (1939), 71–102, especially 82–83; R. R. Betts, "Some Political Ideas of the Early Czech Reformers," *Slavonic and East European Review,* XXXI (1952–53), 20–35. [The two articles by Betts are reprinted in his *Essays in Czech History* (London: Athlone Press, 1969), pp. 132–59, 63–85, respectively. See also Howard Kaminsky, "The University of Prague in the Hussite Revolution: The Role of the Masters," in *Universities in Politics,* ed. J. W. Baldwin & R. A. Goldthwaite (Baltimore: Johns Hopkins University Press, 1972), pp. 79–106.]

[4] The MS. of *De Veris Universalibus* is in possession of the Royal Library in Stockholm (*Kungliga Biblioteket*). The explicit reads as follows: "Explicit tractatus de veris universalibus magistri venerabilis Joh. Wycleph, sacre theologie veri et magni professoris, a. D. 1398 in die s. Jeronimi Slawy per manus Hus de Hussynecz. Amen tak bóh day." In F. M. Bartoš, *Literární činnost M. J. Husi* (Praha: Ceska Akademie ved a umeni, 1948), p. 132.

[5] Palacký, *Documenta,* p. 161.

In his *Super IV Sententiarum* Hus says: "Hec propter illos disserui, qui iudicio temerario Magistrum Johannem Wiclef certitudinaliter asserunt et predicant esse dampnatum eternaliter in inferno. Ego autem a temerario volens declinare iudicio, spero, quod sit de numero salvandorum. Et si est in celo, laudetur gloriosus Dominus, qui eum ibi constituit; si in purgatorio, liberet eum misericors Dominus cicius; si in inferno, maneat in eterno supplicio ex Dei iusto iudicio." Vaclav Flajšhans and Marie Komínková, eds., *Magistri Joannis Hus Opera Omnia, Vol. II: Super IV. Sententiarum* (Prague: Vilimek, 1903–27), p. 621.

⁶ Palacký, *Documenta*, p. 168.

The translation of the Czech verbs *zwiklati* and *wiklati*, used by Hus to describe the effects of Wyclyf's teaching on the clergy, presents difficulties. The meaning of the two verbs was never satisfactorily established. They can be translated by the English verbs: to swing, to make loose, to make dizzy, to confuse, to perplex. Palacký translates by the Latin *vacillare*. Odlozilik, *Wyclif and Bohemia*, p. 33, translates Hus's marginal remark in the above mentioned Stockholm MS. of *De Veris Universalibus* in which the verb occurs in the following way: "O Wyclif, Wyclif, it won't be only one man's head that you will turn."

⁷ Palacký, *Documenta*, p. 184.

The absolute dependence of Hus on Wyclyf was "established" by Johann Loserth, *Huss und Wiclif. Zur Genesis der hussitischen Lehre*, 2nd ed. rev. (Muenchen: Oldenbourg, 1925). In Czech historical literature Loserth's views have never been accepted in full. A scholarly refusal was presented by Vaclav Novotny, *Nabozenske hnuti ceske ve 14. a 15. stoleti* [Czech religious movement in the fourteenth and fifteenth centuries] (Prague: Otto, 1915). In the Anglo-Saxon world isolated voices raised objections too. See David Brown, "Wiclif and Hus," *British and Foreign Evangelical Review*, XXXIII (1884), 572–78. John Neville Figgis also recognized different strains in the two reformers: "Wyclif was as much superior to Hus as an original thinker, as he was his inferior in personal charm. Hus was the most lovable of men." In "John Wyclif," *Typical English Churchmen* (London: SPCK, 1909), Series II, pp. 3–46. Henri Hauser speaks of "le doux Jean Hus" in *La naissance du protestantisme* (Paris: Presses Universitaires de France, 1940), p. 31. A strong rebuttal of Loserth's thesis has been published by Matthew Spinka, *John Hus and the Czech Reform* (Chicago: The University of Chicago Press, 1941). [S. H. Thomson's objections to the notions of Loserth concerning the heavy dependence of Hus upon Wyclyf are noted in his edition of *Magistri Johannis Hus Tractatus de Ecclesia* (Boulder: University of Colorado Press, 1958), pp. viii–xi, xxxii–xxxiv. The attitude of Hus towards the views of Wyclyf are noticed also in Matthew Spinka, *John Hus* (Princeton: Princeton University Press, 1968), pp. 58–9, 112–13, 158–60. Spinka's continuing rejection of the ideas of Loserth may be found in his *John Hus' Concept of the Church* (Princeton: Princeton University Press, 1966), pp. 4 (". . . the biased and warped judgments of such men as Johann Loserth . . ."), 65–6, 112–13, 253–5. And see in particular Paul de Vooght, *L'hérésie de Jean Huss* 2nd ed. (Louvain: Publications Universitaires de Louvain, 1975).]

⁸ Hermann von der Hardt, ed., *Magnum Oecumenicum Constantiense Concilium de Universali Ecclesiae Reformatione, Unione, et Fide*, 7 vols. (Helmstadt: Genschius, 1696–1742), IV, col. 751. "Ad *vicesimum quintum* articulum respondit, quod in camera sua fecit depingi doctores Philosophorum, inter quos tanquam Philosophi fuit imago *Johannis Wicleff*, non tamen cum diademate in capite."

⁹ "Credo in Wykleph, ducem inferni, patronum Boemi, et in Hus, filium eius unicum, nequam nostrum, quo conceptus est ex spiritu Luciperi, natus matre eius et factus incarnatus equalis Wikleph secundum malam voluntatem et maior secundum eius persecucionem, regnans tempore desolationis studii Pragensis, tempore, quo Boemia a fide apostatavit. Qui propter nos hereticos descendit ad inferna et non resurget a mortuis nec habebit vitam eternam. Amen."

The *Sanctus* was parodied in the following way: "Planctus, planctus, planctus canimus, Wykleph Scarioth; pleni sunt celi et terra heresi tua." This interesting document is discussed by Zdenek Nejedlý, *Dějiny husitského zpěvu* [The History of Hussite Religious Chant], 2d ed., 5 vols. (Prague: Ceskoslovenska akademie ved, 1954–55), III, 373–4.

[10] A convenient edition of the forty-five articles is in Henricus Denzinger, *Enchiridion Symbolorum Definitionum et Declarationum de Rebus Fidei et Morum,* ed. Carolus Rahner, S.J., 30th ed. (Freiburg i.B.: Herder, 1955), pars. 581–625. The *diffusa condemnatio* is in Hardt, *Oecumenicum Constantiense Concilium,* III, cols. 212–335. [A recent discussion of the condemnation is E. C. Tatnall, "The Condemnation of John Wyclif at the Council of Constance," *Studies in Church History,* VII (1971), 209–18.]

[11] Bernard Gui, *Manuel de l'Inquisiteur,* ed. and tr. G. Mollat, Les classiques de l'histoire de France au moyen âge, 2 vols. (Paris: Champion, 1926–27), I, lx. Emil Friedberg, ed., *Corpus Iuris Canonici,* 2 vols., 2d ed. (Leipzig: Tauchnitz, 1881), II, cols. 553 and 779–780: Decretales Gregorii IX, lib. III, tit. XXVIII, De sepulturis, cap. XII, Sacris, and lib. V, tit. VII, De haereticis, cap. VIII, Sicut.

[12] Nicolaus Eymeric, *Directorium Inquisitorum,* ed. Franciscus Peña (Rome, 1585), pp. 615–621. Quaestio XLIII: An Inquisitor *possit procedere contra mortuos.*

[13] The part played by the English Church in the fall of Richard II has been excellently analysed by Ludwig Flathe, *Geschichte der Vorläeufer der Reformation,* 2 vols. (Leipzig: Goeschen, 1835–36), II, 166 and 185. Flathe recognized the fact that the English royal house sided with the reformers, sc. the Lollards, in their effort to reform, and thus weaken the position of the Church in England. He then described the reaction of the English hierarchy: "Darum wird die Kirche, um in der Sprache dieser Zeit zu reden, revolutionaer. Sie stürzet das Koenigliche Geschlecht, welches den Lollardismus zu begünstigen scheint, und stellt ein anderes auf, welches ihn verfolgen soll. Immer nur unter einer Bedingung ist der hierarchiche Geist ein Stützpunct der Throne, dass diese sich wiederum ihm unbedingt fügen, sich nicht herausbewegen aus dem Kreise, mit dem sie von ihm umzogen worden. Ging die Revolution, auf welche hier gedeutet wird, der Sturz des Königs Richard II, auch keinesweges allein aus der Kirche hervor, so hatte sie doch einen starken Antheil an derselben und sie war in ihrem Wunsche und in ihrem Geiste" (II, 168).

[14] Walsingham, *Historia Anglicana,* II, 328. [See K. B. McFarlane, *Lancastrian Kings and Lollard Knights* (Oxford: Clarendon Press, 1972).]

[15] This view has been recently endorsed by a Polish writer: "Through his [Netter's] perception and understanding of dialectics, this polemic of genius, exegesist, theologian and fearless exterminator of Wiklef's heresy, fully succeeded in exposing Wiklef's errors and sophistry, and, in fighting against them by means of arguments drawn from the Bible and the Church Fathers, proved their weakness and lack of fairness." (Translated from Polish by Miss Irena Zamorska of the School of Slavonic and East European Studies, London.) In KS. M. Lech Kaczmarek, *Tomasz Netter-Waldensis jako obronca prymatu sw. Piotra, Studium dogmatyczno-hostoryczne* ("Poznanskie Towarzystwo przyjaciol nauk: Prace Komisji Teologiczne," Vol. III, Part I; Poznan, 1947), p. 5. [For further comments on Netter, see M. Hurley, "'Scriptura sola': Wyclif and his Critics," *Traditio,* XVI (1960), 277–9.]

[16] "Scripturus iuvante deo contra novellos haereticos Witclevistas, qui his novissimis diebus Anglicanas repleverunt ecclesias & hodie totam invasere Bohemiam: ex ipsis radicibus fidei quid Christus, quid apostoli eius, quid post eos sancti patres & doctores ab initio crediderunt & suo tempore docuerunt, propono certiores facere credentes." Thomas Netter Waldensis, *Doctrinale fidei ecclesiae catholicae contra Witclevistas & Hussitas,* 3 vols. (Paris, 1532–57), I, fols. 2v–34.

[17] Thomas Gascoigne, *Loci e libro veritatum,* ed. James E. Thorold Rogers (Oxford: Clarendon Press, 1881), p. 137.

[18] Reginald Pecock, *The Repressor of Over Much Blaming of the Clergy,* ed. Churchill Babington, 2 vols. (London: "Rolls Series," 1860), 11, 413.

[19] Rudolf Urbanek, *Vek Podebradsky* [The Age of George of Podebradsky], Vol. III, Part I of *Ceske Dejiny* [History of Bohemia], ed. Vaclav Novotny (Prague: Laichter, 1915), p. 825.

[20] Johannis de Ragusio, *Tractatus de reductione Bohemorum,* ed. F. Palacký, 3 vols. ("Monumenta Conciliorum Generalium Seculi Decimi Quinti. Concilium Basileense";

Wien, 1857–1932), I, 269, 270, 272. For the Czechs and Peter Payne, Wyclyf was "doctor evangelicus." [On this general subject, see W. R. Cook, "John Wyclif and Hussite Theology, 1415–1436," *Church History*, XLII (1973), 335–49.]

[21] Petr Chelčický, *Sit viry* [The Net of Faith], ed. Emil Smetanka (Prague: Comenium, 1912), pp. 62, 64, 82, 94, 96, 139, 239. On Chelčický see Peter Brock, *Political and Social Doctrine of the Czech Brethren in the Fifteenth and Early Sixteenth Centuries* (The Hague: Mouton, 1957), pp. 25–69 *passim*.

[22] English text in Henry Bettenson, ed., *Documents of the Christian Church* (London: Oxford University Press, 1943), pp. 189–190.

[23] Aeneas Silvius (Pius II), "Chronica Boemorum" (*Opera Omnia*; Basel, 1579), pp. 223–264.

[24] Lollardy was by no means extinguished. The burning of Joan Boughton in 1495 might have been an isolated case, but as the facts demonstrate, Joan had faithful followers: "Upon the xxviii daye of apryll was an old cankyrd heretyke that dotid ffor age namyd Johanne Bowghton wedowe & modyr unto the wyffe of sir John yong, which dowgthyr as soom Reportid had a grete smell of an heretyk aftyr the modyr; Brent In Smythffeeld, This woman was iiij score yeris of age or more and held viij oppynyons of heresy whych I passe ovyr, ffor the heryng of theym is nothyr plesaunt nor ffruteffull, She was a dyscypyll of wyclyff whom she accomptid ffor a Seynt, and held soo ffast & ffermly viij of his xij oppynyons that alle the doctors of london cowde not turn hyr ffrom oon of theym, and when It was told to hir that she shuld be brent ffor hyr obstynacy & ffals byleve, She set nowght at theyr wordis but deffyed theym, ffor she said she was soo belovid wyth God & his holy angelys, That all the ffyre in london shuld not hurt hyr, But upon the morw a quarteron of ffagot wyth a ffewe Rede consumyd hir in a lytill while . . . . But it apperyd that she lafft soom of hyr dyscyplys behynd hyr, ffor the nyght ffolowyng the more part of the asshys of that ffyre that she was brent In, were hadd awaye, and kepyd ffor a precious Relyk, In an erthyn pott, as afftyr was provid In the tyme of sir Henry Colett beyng mayer, ..." A. H. Thomas and I. D. Thornley, eds., *The Great Chronicle of London* (London: Printed by George W. Jones for the Library Committee of the Corporation of the City of London, 1938), pp. 252–3.

[25] See J. Huizinga, *The Waning of the Middle Ages* (New York: Anchor-Doubleday, 1954), pp. 138–51. There is an excellent discussion in Hellmut Rosenfeld, *Der mittelalterliche Totentanz. Entstehung-Entwicklung-Bedeutung* ("Beihefte zum Archiv fuer Kulturgeschichte," eds. Herbert Grundmann and Fritz Wagner, Heft 3; Muenster: Boehlau, 1954). The pictorial representation of the dance of death appeared on the walls of St. Paul's Cathedral in 1440. *Ibid.*, p. 170.

[26] Hartmann Schedel, *Libri Cronicarum* (Nuernberg, 1493), fol. cclxiiii r. [It has not been possible to confirm this citation.]

[27] *Ibid.*, fols. ccxxxviii r–ccxl r.

[28] Johannes Trithemius, *Catalogus scriptorum ecclesiasticorum* . . . (Cologne, 1531), fol. cxxxvii v.

[29] *Ibid.*, fols. cxix r and cxxxvii v. [The quotation is from the latter.]

[30] *Ibid.*, fol. cxviii v. Archbishop Fitzralph did not always belong to the *bona fide* Catholic writers. Cardinal Bellarmin was of the opinion that "Hic auctor [Fitzralph] caute valde legendus est, praesertim libro 10, contra Armenos cap. 4. & cap. 23. & 24. & lib. ii. cap. 4. & sermone primo & quarto, in quibus locis multos errores habet de potestate Presbyterorum, de paupertate Christi, & de statu Religiosorum Mendicantium: consulat lector Thoman Valdensem, qui errores Armachani & Joan. Wiclefi, qui ab Armachano aliqua accepit, diligenter refutat: consulat etiam, si placet, quae nos scripsimus lib. de Monachis cap. 45. & 46." Robert Cardinal Bellarmin, *De Scriptoribus Ecclesiasticis Liber Unus* . . . (Cologne, 1684), p. 223.

[31] A comparative study of the doctrines of Wyclyf and Luther is still to be written. A recent, but limited examination has been presented by Martin Schmidt, "John Wyclifs Kirchenbegriff. Der Christus humilis Augustins bei Wyclif. Zugleich ein Beitrag zur Frage: Wyclif und Luther," *Gedenkschrift fuer D. Werner Elert*. Beitraege zur historischen und systematischen Theologie, ed. Friedrich Huebner, Wilhelm Maurer, and

Ernst Kinder (Berlin: Lutherisches Verlaghaus, 1955), pp. 72–108 *passim*. [Arguments for placing Wyclyf in the context of later reforms are presented in John Stacey, *John Wyclif and Reform* (Philadelphia: Westminster Press, 1964).]

[32] Roland H. Bainton, *Here I Stand, A Life of Martin Luther* (New York: Mentor-The New American Library, 1955), p. 89.

[33] *Ibid.*, p. 92.

[34] *Ibid.*, p. 89–90.

[35] "Or Sleidan commence son histoire au temps de Leon dixiesme, & *ment gentiment* [Italics added] tout á l'entree de son histoire en telle sorte toutesfois, que cela luy est commun avec tous ceux qui sont de telle farine que luy: . . . ." Gabriel Du Préau, *Histoire de l'estat et succès de l'Église* . . . 12 vols. (Paris, 1583), II, 360 r.

[36] "Sive Mentelius est, sive Gutenbergius, sive alius inventor; plus commodi ingenio suo ad communem utilitatem tulit, quam vel Columbus aut Americus novi Orbis pervestigatione." Christophorus Cellarius, *Historia medii aevi a temporibus Constantini Magni ad Constantinopolim a Turcis captam deducta* . . . (Jena, 1698), p. 229.

[37] In 1487 Pope Innocent VIII universally prescribed the censorship of books and entrusted the bishops with its execution. The Congregation of the Index was called into existence by Pius IV in 1571.

[38] "Venit nunc scriptura in manus omnium. Idiotae, prophani, mulierculae, etiam de questionibus difficillimis, iudicium adhibent, etiam de praedestinatione dei, de gratia, & libero arbitrio, & aliis, in quibus altissima desudaverunt ingenia, & oberrarunt." Ambrosius Catharinus, O.P., *Speculum Haereticorum* (Cracoviae, 1540), sign. Bvv.

[39] Claudius Coussord, *Valdensium ac quorundam aliorum errores, praecipuas, ac pene omnes, quae nunc vigent, haereseis continentes* (Paris, 1548), p. 79 r. [On Wyclyf as a translator of the Bible, see P. A. Knapp, "John Wyclif as Bible Translator: The Texts for the English Sermons," *Speculum*, XLVI (1971), 713–20.]

[40] The *Doctrinale* with its component parts *De Sacramentis* and *De Sacramentalibus* was first published in Paris in 1532. The next edition was that of Salamanca in 1556–7. The last sixteenth-century edition was published in Venice in 1571.

[41] I have used several editions of this very popular sixteenth-century work. The earliest edition available in the British Library is that of 1522 in which the place of publication is Cologne. The other two editions which I have examined were published in Cologne in 1537 and 1523 respectively. The edition of 1537 is advertised on the title page as *editio quinta, nunc ab ipso auctore & aucta & recognita*. The edition of 1523, on the other hand, is announced as *editio secunda priore multo emaculatior & locupletior, nempe ab ipso nunc aucta & recognita*.

[42] Bernardus de Lutzenburgo, *Catalogus Haereticorum* . . . (Cologne, 1523), sign. H viii v.

[43] Bernardus de Lutzenburgo, *Catalogus Haereticorum* . . . (Cologne, 1522), sign. a iii r and a iii v.

[44] *Ibid.*, sign. b i v. Gotfridus Trano, who died in 1245, was author of the *Summa super rubricis decretalium*. According to Schulte, "De Summe ist . . . das verbreitetse und gelesenste Buch geworden." See Johann Friedrich von Schulte, *Die Geschichte der Quellen und Literatur des Canonischen Rechts*, 3 vols., reprint of 1875 ed. (Graz: Akademische Druck- und Verlagsanstalt, 1956), II, 88–91.

[45] Bernardus de Lutzenburgo, *Catalogus Haereticorum* . . . (Cologne, 1523), sign. H v r.

[46] Bernardus de Lutzenburgo, *Catalogus Haereticorum* . . . (Cologne, 1537), sign. T (6) r.

[47] Johann Fabri, *Wie sich Johannis Huszs, der Pickarder, und Joannis vo Wessalia Leren und Buecher mit Martino Luther vergleichen* (Leipzig, 1528), sign. A i v and A ii r.

[48] Joannes Cochlaeus, *Warhafftige Historia von Magister Johan Hussen von anfang seiner newen Sect bisz zum ende seines lebens ym Concilio zu Constnitz* . . . (Leipzig, 1547), F 3 r. [Cochlaeus, John Bale, Thomas Fuller, John Foxe, and others attracted the attention of M. E. Aston, "John Wycliffe's Reformation Reputation," *Past and*

Present, No. 30 (1965), 23–51. Another important contribution to Wyclyf historiography is James Crompton, "John Wyclif: A Study in Mythology," *Transactions of the Leicestershire Archaeological and Historical Society,* XLII (1966–7), 6–34. Crompton significantly wrote: ". . . a useful book could be written about the errors and misconceptions that later generations have associated with the name of the rector of Lutterworth" (p. 8).]

[49] Cochlaeus expressed several times his admiration for Bohemia. In the *Historiae Hussitarum* he described it as "florentissimum regnum" and explained that he compiled the material for his work "in laudem & gloriam Inclytae Nationis, ac fortissimae Gentis Bohemorum . . . ." Without denying that Hus was a heretic, he was moved—by motives which are unknown—to characterize him as "infoelix Hus." Joannes Cochlaeus, *Historiae Hussitarum libri duodecim* . . . (Mainz, 1549), pp. 15, 502, 92.

[50] Coussord, *Valdensium . . . errores,* p. 56 r.

[51] John Bale, *Illustrium maioris Britanniae scriptorum, hoc est, Angliae, Cambriae, ac Scotiae summarium* . . . (Ipswich, 1548).

[52] These complaints appeared in a short biographical note of John Leland written in 1549 by John Bale. The latter was shocked by indifference displayed by his countrymen to their past: "Amonge all the nacions in whome I have wandered, for the knowledge of thynges . . . I have founde nene so negligent and untoward, as I have found England in the due serch of theyr auncyent hystoryes, to the syngulare fame and bewtye thereof." [The quotations have not been confirmed.]

[53] Bale, *Summarium,* pp. 154 v–155 r.

[54] *Ibid.,* pp. 155 r, 157 v.

[55] John Leland, *Collectanea de rebus Britannicis,* ed. Thomas Hearne, 6 vols. (Oxford, 1774), II, 409. According to Horne Wyclyf suffered a stroke on St. Innocent's Day, that is on 28 December 1384. Walsingham places the stroke on 29 December 1385— "Die Sancti Thomas, Cantuariensis Archiepiscopi et Martyris . . . ." Walsingham, *Historia Anglicana,* II, 119–120.

[56] John Bale, *Scriptorum illustrium maioris Brytannie, quam nunc Angliam & Scotiam vocant: Catalogus* . . . (Basel, 1557), pp. 450, 456.

[57] The first English edition of the *Actes and Monuments* was preceded by the *Commentarii rerum in ecclesia gestarum* . . . published in Strasbourg in 1554 during Foxe's exile. The work shows unmistakable traces of Bale's influence. Bale's terminology is fully accepted: Wyclyf is "stella matutina" and "vir pius." Bale's text is, however, improved by the inclusion of documents which form the backbone of the narrative. (The two quotations are on fols. 2 v and 9 r). [The ties between Bale and Foxe have been more recently noticed by M. E. Aston, "Lollards and the Reformation: Survival or Revival?" *History,* XLIX (1964), 164–9.]

[58] John Foxe, *Actes and Monuments of These Latter and Perillous Dayes Touching Matters of the Church* . . . (London: John Day, 1563), p. 98.

[59] *Ibid.,* p. 85.

[60] *Ibid.,* p. 88.

[61] *Ibid.,* p. 90.

[62] *Ibid.,* pp. 89–106.

[63] Thomas Walsingham's chronicle was printed for the first time in London in 1574.

[64] John Foxe, *The First Volume of the Ecclesiasticall History, Contayning the Actes and Monumentes of Thinges Passed in Every Kinges Time* . . . (London: John Daye, 1576), p. 420.

[65] *Ibid.,* p. 421.

[66] *Idem.*

[67] Johannes Dubravius, *Historiae regni Boiemiae* . . . (Prostannae [Prostejov in Moravia], 1552), Epistola nuncupatoria.

[68] *Ibid.,* fol. cxlvii r.

[69] Daniel Adam of Veleslavín, *Kalendar Hystorycky* [An Historical Calendar], 2d ed. (Prague, 1590), Dedication.

[70] *Ibid.,* genealogical table.

[71] *Ibid.*, pp. 369, 388, 635.

[72] Ioannes de Turrecremata, *Summa de ecclesia* (Venice, 1561). The work was written in 1448–9. The *editio princeps* appeared in 1480. Turrecremata asserted that both the Valdensians and Wyclyf claimed "quod solum apud sanctos viros essent claves ecclesiae." *Ibid.*, fol. 217 v.

[73] Alphonsus à Castro Zamorensi, "Adversus omnes haereses libri quatuordecim" in *Opera* (Paris, 1571), col. 94.

[74] *Ibid.*, cols. 70, 79.

[75] *Ibid.*, col. 70. See also col. 371.

[76] *Ibid.*, col. 154.

[77] *Ibid.*, cols. 184, 185, 238, 240, 303, 325, 368, 371, 379, 507, 557, 578, 585, 698, 824, 888, 897, 940, 961, 944, 997.

[78] *Ibid.*, col. 798.

[79] *Ibid.*, col. 91.

[80] "Nullus est Ecclesiae status quem non momorderit Ioannes Wicleph, nulla est potestas cui non detraxerit. Nec contentus est ipse obedientiam & subiectionem suis superioribus denegare, nisi etiam subditis id idem faciendum persuaderet. Neque hoc satis esse putavit, nisi subditos superiores suis praelatis, & vasallos superiores suis dominis faceret . . . . Talis est Wicleph, qui ut favorem populi acquireret, in hunc lapsus est vesanum & pestiferum errorem, quo nullus alius pestilentior esse posset . . . . O miseranda talis respublica, que iuxta Wiclephi sententiam gubernanda esset. In ea enim omnes rudes homines, idiote, scelesti, raptores, adulteri, mendaces, prelatos & dominos suos corrigere vellent, & qui peior esset, vehementius dominum & superiorem invaderet, ut ipse a nullo punirentur, sed in sua nequitia impunis manerent. Tunc enim omnia essent confusa. Puer contra senem tumultuaretur, ignobiles surgerent in nobilem, idiotae contra sapientes, discipuli contra magistrum, filii adversus parentes. Et ita esset respublica puteus quidam, vel (ut verius dicam) abyssus scandalorem. Quid non faceret populus tali licentia donatus? Est enim populus fera quaedam & immanissima bestia, qua non est alia ferior aut truculentior." *Ibid.*, col. 964.

[81] Jean Crespin, *La vie de M. Iean Wicleff* (Lyon, 1565). This work, published anonymously (and catalogued in the British Library without author under G 20044.2) is the work, as I have discovered, of Crespin. It is a reprinted part of his larger work based on Foxe's *Commentarii rerum in ecclesia gestarum* . . . and published under the title *Recueil de plusieurs personnes qui ont constamment enduré la mort pour le nom de nostre Seigneur Iesus Christ, depuis Iean Wicleff, & Iean Hus iusques à ceste année presente M.D.LV* in Geneva in 1555, one year after Foxe's *Commentarii*. Crespin was not only an apologist of the Protestant martyrs but also a deeply religious man who realized the tragedy of the split in the Christian family of nations. In the *Recueil* a sigh escaped him: "Y-a-il eu plus grande confusion au monde que celle est maintenant?" *Ibid.*, sign.* 2 v.

[82] Crespin, *La vie*, sign. A ii v.

[83] *Ibid.*, sign. A iii r and v, and A (iv) v.

[84] *Ibid.*, sign. B ii v.

[85] *Ibid.*, sign. C (iv) r.

[86] Gabriel Prateolus Marcossius, *De vitis, sectis, et dogmatibus omnium haereticorum* (Cologne, 1569).

[87] *Ibid.*, Index authorum.

[88] *Ibid.*, p. 226. [The quotation has not been confirmed.]

[89] *Ibid.*, p. 55.

[90] Gabriel Du Préau, *Histoire de l'estat et succès de l'Église, dressée en forme de chronique générale et universelle* . . . (Paris, 1583).

[91] *Ibid.*, fol. 85 r.

[92] *Ibid.*, fols. 128 r, 145 r.

[93] *Ibid.*, fol. 146 r.

[94] Théodore de Bèze, *Icones, id est verae imagines virorum doctrina simul et pietate illustrium* . . . (Geneva, 1580), sign. A ii r.

[95] Théodore de Bèze, *Les vrais pourtraits des hommes illustres en piete et doctrine* . . . , tr. Simon Goulart (Geneva?, 1581), p. 3.

[96] *Ibid.*, p. 4.

D'ou vint ce zele ardant, ce plus qu'humain courage?
  Qui te fit, ô Wiclef, desfier, assaillir
  Celuy qui d'un clin d'oeil faisoit tout tressaillir,
  Et qui tenoit l'Europe en si cruel servage?
Dieu t'arma pour piquer de l'Antechrist la rage:
  Alaigre tu l'assaus le premier, sans faillir
  D'un coup bien asseuré le sang tu fais iaillir,
  A ton los immortel, à son deuil & dommage.
Sitost que l'eus frapé, la mort le menassa:
  Ce moqueur s'en moquoit, mais sentant en son ame
  Un feu continuel, pour l'estaindre il pensa
Qu'il faloit sans delay te ietter dans la flamme.
  Mais en bruslant tes os es cendres a laissé
  Le feu, dont à la mort il est ores pressé.

See these lines written by *Delta*, "On the Portrait of Wicliffe," *Blackwood's Edinburgh Magazine*, XXVII (January–June, 1830), 110–111.

I love to trace the lines of that face, [Wyclyf's]
So calm, yet so commanding;
Thy white beard's venerable grace
O'er thy russet vest expanding;
Thine eyebrows so deeply arch'd—thy look
Of serenest contemplation,
At whose kindling glance the guilty shook
In pitiful consternation.

[97] Sebastianus Medicis, *Summa omnium haeresum et Catalogus Schismaticorum, haereticorum et idolatrarum* (Florence, 1581). The change of tone is best exemplified in Medicis's treatment of *subditus. Ibid.*, p. 431.

[98] Robert Abbot, *A Mirrour of Popish Subtilties* (London, 1594), p. 172.

Chapter
58803
2

The Seventeenth Century

The new century was scarcely established in its course when Nicolas Vignier—by profession *medicin & historiographe* of Henry III of France—published a book whose spirit pointed to the future, and to the appearance of Bayle's famous *Dictionary*.[1] Vignier, who (or it might have been his publisher) affixed to every page of the thick folio volume the confident words *La vraye histoire de l'église,* displayed similar traits as a precursor of the Enlightenment. The use of subtle irony, the attempt to reduce religious arguments to the rule of reason, the sympathy for the independent thinker couched in terms which did not inflict mortal wounds but pricked the sensitive skin—all these literary qualities are in constant view, and contribute to an impression of detachment from the heat of the religious battle, and contemplation of burning issues with impassive calm. Vignier, unusually well informed about the life of Wyclyf, began his portrayal of Wyclyf from the time of his dispute with the Carmelite Cunningham, which he assigned to 1371.[2] He emphasized the fact that Wyclyf "estoit estimé le premier des Theologiens de son temps," and accounted for the sympathy of the great nobles by the exemplary life he led—one not contrary to his doctrine. The trials of Wyclyf—which he orders in better chronological sequence than John Lewis—and his opposition to the friars were prominently mentioned in the text.[3] The existence and activities of the friars evidently irritated Vignier. Writing about the attacks of the mendicants on Fitzralph and Ughtred of Boldon, he gave vent to his resentment in the following quasi-Voltarian way:

La corruption des moeurs & la licence de malfaire estoit si grande en ce siecle, que les Prebstres & moines osoient impudemment prendre & violer les femmes & nonnains: Tellement qu'il y eut quelques vierges occises par eux qui ne vouloient satisfaire à leurs impudicitez. Plusiers aussi d'entre eux faisoient entendre aux femmes, que c'estoit moindre peché de paillarder avec eux, qu'avec les lais; mesmement qu'ils avoient puissance de les ab-

25

souldre de toutes leurs fautes: D'avantage que coucher avec eux en l'absence de leurs maris, les preservoit & guerissoit de plusiers maladies. Lesquels abus a repris Iehan Wiclef en son livre de l'hypocrisie.[4]

Of a different tone is the work which was published in Ingolstadt in 1601 by Cardinal Robert Bellarmin.[5] Today the author of *De controversiis christianae fidei, adversus huius temporis haereticos* is remembered, if at all, in conjunction with Galileo rather than with Wyclyf or the sacrament of the Eucharist. In a text of 6031 folio columns, Bellarmin discussed heretical tenets held by Christians in the past. Bellarmin presented the unorthodox utterances of the heretics *sine ira et studio*—if the reader accepts the Catholic point of view as the only correct one. He does not indulge in poisonous epithets, his temperature does not seem to rise, and we enjoy an uninterrupted flow of calm reasoning. Bellarmin is thoroughly convinced of the unimpeachable character of the Church's condemnations, and he lets the record speak for itself.

De Controversiis is a running commentary on the heresies of the past, but in many cases the commentary is not his. In the case of Wyclyf, Netter's *Doctrinale* served Bellarmin as the key to the condemned articles of Wyclyf at the eighth session of the Council of Constance, and with Netter's arguments he confounds the English heretic.[6] But Bellarmin did not depend entirely on Netter. He knew, for example, that before the time of Wyclyf the friars were exposed to attacks from William of Saint Amour, Desiderius Langobardus, Gerard of Abbéville, and Archbishop Fitzralph.[7] This fact was well known already in the ''age of Wyclyf'' but it is always refreshing to find historical names among dogmatic infinitudes.[8] Now and then the cardinal adduced his own evidence to arrive at a conclusion which because of the changing times had been inaccessible to Netter. Speaking of the Eucharist, he formulated the question and then gave the answer as follows:

> First we would ask whether God would have been able, being truly present, to set forth the body and blood of the Lord in the form of bread and wine. Then, would that have been his wish.
> On the first question John Wyclyf (upon Thomas Netter of Walden, book 2, chapters 72–3) and his disciple John Calvin clearly deny that this could happen.[9]

Under the same heading of Eucharist, Bellarmin discussed the sources of Wyclyf's teaching on the sacrament and proved to his audience that the man who was most influential on Wyclyf in this respect was Rupert of Deutz (Rupert Tuitensis). The latter's *De divinis officiis,* a work which was and still is for the Wyclyf scholar *sine honore et titulo,* Bellarmin summarized as follows:

> Rupert therefore has taught that the bread of the Eucharist is transubstantiated by the Word, in the same way that human nature is transformed by the same Word . . . . The same author in book 2, chapter 2 of *De divinis officiis* teaches the same thing at length: where he declares that the bread itself becomes the body of Christ, not because it is changed into the flesh of the Lord, but because it is transubstantiated by the Word. From which it follows that the bread is the body of Christ, but not a human body, nor flesh, but a panacea; and far different from that which was born of the Virgin. In the same place he teaches that these two bodies can be called one, because one has taken the place of both, or Christ is the one who has become both: and he says in eloquent words that those bodies, the sanctified bread and the flesh, are one, because the same Christ on high, that is, in heaven, is in the flesh, on earth, that is, on the altar, in the bread.[10]

Bellarmin was well received even in England. The keeper of the Bodleian Library, Thomas James, wrote in 1608 that Bellarmin was "the most aged, and iudicious Jesuit at this day in al Christendome."[11] He wrote this sentence in the course of his defence of Wyclyf, then assailed by two Jesuits: Father Parsons and Gretser, "that upstart Goliath."[12] The need for vindicating Wyclyf before the eyes of the religious world was obvious indeed. The question which for a long time all the sincere Anglicans had on their lips was: What are we going to do with Wyclyf? Is he going to remain a heretic even for the Church which has once and for all repudiated the Pope? The uneasiness of the Anglican divine of the more discriminating type—a class to which Bale did not belong—was rather growing than disappearing when the name of Wyclyf had to be met face to face.[13] It fell to Thomas James to present to the Anglicans a purified John Wyclyf; to do so it was necessary, as the title of his tiny tract says, to show his conformity with the Church of England. The first sentence, rolling in sonorous language fit for the pomp and circumstance of the moment, is designed to dispel any doubts as to Wyclyf's Anglican orthodoxy:

> Whereas among al the writers, which have since the daies of Antichrist sharpened there pens in defence of the Gospel, and maintained the cause of Christ against Antichrist and his Supposts, by opposing themselves as Arch-pillers, against the Arch-hereticks and Caterpillers of there times: there is none that hath behaved himselfe more religiously, valiantlie, learnedlie, and constantlie, then this stout Champion, reverend Doctor, & worthie preacher of Gods word Iohn Wickliffe . . . .[14]

These introductory words set the tone. This "worthie instrument & chosen vessel of Gods glorie,"[15] we get the indelible impression, was always right, and with the assistance of James the puzzling problems were reduced to simple and straightforward propositions. Wyclyf never was a papist: ''he preached against the pretiosity, speciosity, and miraculositie, and sundry other sophistications about images''; ''he held the riches and goods of Christians not to be common, as touching the right, title, and possession (as the Anabaptists now, & a certaine Bald Priest in his time did hold) notwithstanding, by a Christian charitie, they were to be made common, as he teacheth.''[16] James noted that Wyclyf prayed to the Virgin Mary but did not forget to note that he later changed his attitude.[17] James also stated that Wyclyf was not for the confiscation of Church property in general but only of that part which belonged to the friars, and he denied that he was against the correction of princes by the people since he did ''stoutly and valiantly maintaine the kings Supremacie.''[18] The list of Wyclyf's good properties has virtually no end. In one word: Wyclyf already had fought the Reformation. Those who smeared him or his views found no quarter with the librarian: ''Walsingham was a Lyar.'' Netter had neither truth nor honesty in his words, and Master Stow—here spoke undeniably the Oxford University intellectual—''was a painefull Citizen, by trade a Taylour, by his industrie a Chronicler.''[19] Moreover, Stow could not speak Latin. Thomas James, of course, could. His apology is supported throughout by passages from *De Veritate Sacrae Scripturae,* a work which Thomas James was the first to expound in detail before the nineteenth century.[20] The tract has an appendix where James tried, it seems as an afterthought, to outline the basic facts of Wyclyf's life, but we are not introduced to new factual knowledge. James repeated the chronicles that he was born in the North where, as he added, ''some of his name and family (as I understand by others) doe yet remain.''[21] We learn the genealogy of his precursors and masters, and we find Wyclyf in the company of Ockham, Bradwardine, Marsilius, Guide S. Amore [sic], Abelard, *Armachanus* and Grosseteste, an association which cannot be disputed without splitting very fine academic hairs.[22] The Wyclyf scholar may also read for the first time that he was close to King Richard, ''whose Chaplaine he appeared to have beene.''[23] It seems obvious that already in 1608 a truly historical biography of Wyclyf could have been written if the scattered pieces of information had been gathered and viewed as a whole. However, this did not happen for one hundred more years. The seventeenth century was the century of polemics, and where arguments are flying to and fro, history has no props on which to build its narrative.[24]

Gretser, of whom we have heard in James's unflattering remark, was in the latter's eyes ''a young Jesuit.''[25] Did the adjective have any particular meaning? Did James recognize a difference between sixteenth-century and seventeenth-century Jesuits? Had they changed in the lifetime of James? Probably they had, and the innocuous adjective "young" is pregnant with significance. One does not have to read all the 3494 columns of Gretser's defence of the aging Cardinal Bellarmin to realize one has entered a new world.[26] Urbane prose and fair documentation have vanished, replaced by the aggressive tenacity of a writer who strives for the defeat of his opponent by any means.

Gretser was especially concerned with the arguments of the Dutch theologian Junius. The latter denied the veracity of the article six condemned at Constance, saying *Deus debet diabolo obedire,* and pointed out that a similar sentence did not exist in any work of Wyclyf which was then available in the libraries. His second complaint was that the Council of Constance falsely attributed the article to Wyclyf.[27] It was Gretser's task to deny the validity of Junius's statements. First, the Jesuit writer pointed out that very few of Wyclyf's works were extant. He then admitted that the condemned sentence was not "in operibus Wiclephi, quae publicata sunt," but failed to recognize how anyone would dare to deny that it existed at one time in the libraries.[28] He came back again to the initial statement and repeated that very few of his works were known to exist. But it was only a tactical retreat because with the next question he ended the possibility of a further discussion. For who then could have found suitable reply to these words: "Et ut omnia superessent, potuisset tamen Haeresiarcha ille, blasphemiae illius magnitudine vel fero offensus, eam ex scriptis suis eradere, ut Melanchthonem & Lutherum erasisse constant"?[29] After the successful parry of the first objection, Gretser had very little trouble with the second one: the Council fathers knew Wyclyf better than a "nudius-tertius exortus Praedicans."[30] But Gretser had not yet finished his attack on Wyclyf and the sixth article, in subsequent times so much debated and invariably found so difficult to explain. He brought into the controversy Luther (who had endorsed the twenty-fifth article) and drew from this isolated act the conclusion that thereby Luther endorsed all forty-five, including the sixth. And how could Junius dispute the authorship of Wyclyf when it was accepted both by Luther and Hus?[31] Gretser deprecated Wyclyf's translation of the Bible and made the reading of it responsible for occult meetings, insolence—even in the minds of women—general contempt of fellow human beings, reluctance to instruction, and incredible haughtiness.[32] There is no doubt in Gretser's mind that Wyclyf was the translator. Did not Hus say it?[33] For once, a heretic was believed.

The Jesuits were not the only order within the Church which attempted to halt the growth of the Lutheran heresy. Melchior Cano, a

Dominican, measured the problem of the split in the Church with a
different eye and a more refined mind than Gretser. Before he became
bishop, Cano was the prefect of the chair of theology at the university
in Salamanca, and applied perceptive and analytic capabilities to the
mission of the Church in his *De locis Theologicis,* regarded even today
as a cornerstone of systematic theological studies. He too stumbled in
his career over Wyclyf, and could not pass him by.[34] Of course his
guide was Netter, but we have from his pen also independent observations, and the one dealing with Wyclyf's notion of predestination is
the most valuable. Cano was disturbed above all by the possibility,
emphasized by Wyclyf, that some pope might be a reprobate and
would have no power over the faithful *nisi forte a Caesare.*[35] He asserted in conformity with the canons of the Church that Wyclyf's view
was opposed and then passed judgment on Wyclyf's opinion in the
form of a question which, as formulated, allowed evasion from its
common-sense logic only by the possible use of superficial verbal virtuosity. Cano went to the core of the problem of predestination when
he asserted: "Quantum vero schismatum quotidie in ecclesia videre-
mus, dum unus alteri diceret, Tu non es de ecclesia, quia malus es:
ego de ecclesia sum, quia sum bonus?"[36] Cano also had no doubt about
the correct succession of heretics. Luther was a follower of Wyclyf,
his *discipulus,* whom he had followed in many articles of heresy: he
followed him especially in his belief that a lay person could administer
the communion, and that schools of theology were nothing but em-
bodiments of the ignorance of truth and stupid fallacies.[37] Cano's ex-
position is not offensive. He is not a tolerant observer, but when he
writes about heresy in general and Luther in particular he makes it
evident that heresy was too deeply rooted to be eradicated by violent
words.[38] It could, however, be discussed as an academic subject. Such
is the message of Cano's work.

A less refined refutation of Wyclyf was attempted by John Pits (Pit-
seus), an English [Catholic] Doctor of Theology who, forced by the
stress of the times and fortified by his unwillingness to abandon the
Catholic faith, found refuge in France and there the liberty to write.
And he, as so many more refugees experiencing the same plight after
him, lived in the past and in memories. Pits himself did not deny it:

> We men cannot be separated from human emotions. Hence it is fitting,
> considering the iniquity of the present time, that the greater part of my life
> has been spent as an exile in foreign lands. Nevertheless I cannot forget
> the land of my birth, parents and ancestors from whom I sprung, nor can
> I forget those whose glorious accomplishments (*rerum gestarum gloria*) are
> for all time to come a spur and incentive to virtue.[39]

Now writing about *res gestae* is really thinking of history, and to Pits history was not only *veritatis investigatio* but also a literary form which taught about the deserts of the good and showed the punishment of the wicked. Pits, too, wrote his under the patronage of Thomas Netter of Walden, whose merits he summarized in the hagiographic terms "illustrissimus Christi Athleta."[40] His evil spirit was John Bale, and to correct him was to establish truth. The first entry betrays immediately Pits's feelings: "Lelandi Catalogum paulo post longiorem fecit, imo suis foecibus infecit Ioannes Bal, seu Balaeus, de quo quid sentiam, mox dicam."[41] On the next six pages he belittles Bale whom, he remarks, the more simple-minded Englishmen idolized. Pits was of a different opinion: ". . . fuit hereticus Anglus, ab ordine Carmelitarum apostata Monachus, & Sacerdos (salva lectoris reverentia) maritatus."[42] What was deeply irritating to the exile was Bale's *libido calumniandi*. In his works Bale insulted the English [Catholic] doctors; for Wyclyf, on the other hand, he had only unreserved praise.[43] But Pits charges Bale's words "Ipsum (Ioannem Wicleffum) aeternus pater per suum spiritum suscitavit . . . ." were sacriligious, and the world ought to know it.[44] Who was Wyclyf? Bale called him *Wiclef* but he was called by others also Weakbelief or Wickedbeleef.[45] He was a rector of Lutterworth in the diocese of Lincoln, a modest post indeed, but Pits encouraged all his readers to learn all about him in Thomas Walsingham's *Richard II*. And a sigh escaped him: "Sed bone Deus, quot in hoc discursu calumniae, blasphemiae, mendacia, contradictiones, adulationes, & superbae praesumptiones!"[46] And playing with the word Bale with malicious joy, Pits concluded: "Fuit certe Wicleffus magnus Propheta Bal."[47]

The *Relationes Historicae* of Pits, written in 1613 but published six years later, was another catalogue of religious writers similar to those of Trithemius, Volaterranus, and Gesner, to name only a few, who made this kind of work a favorite vehicle of knowledge in the sixteenth and seventeenth centuries.[48] There is little originality in the later ones, which usually only slightly shift emphasis from one writer to another. The heroes of the *Relationes* are all the opponents of Wyclyf the author was able to identify. Thomas Netter of Walden is for Pits the "philosophus acutus" and the greatest mind among the late medieval English thinkers.[49] William Butler labored strenuously against the spreading of the English translation of the Bible and was therefore "vir doctus."[50] Everybody from the ecclesiastical intelligentsia who wrote *contra Wiclefitas* was decorated with a string of adjectives, and one may visualize the disappointment of Pits when he had to write under the name of John Stokes (Stoccus): "non nihil litigiosus."[51]

Did the work discredit Bale? It did; but only where the book was allowed to circulate, and where Bale was never an appreciated author anyway. Did, then, the *Relationes Historicae* affect the Wyclyf tradition at all? At any rate we hear much less of them than of Bale's *Centuriae* which Pits had set out to destroy.

Of greater depth than Pits's *Relationes* were the *Historiae Ecclesiasticae* of the Polish Dominican Abraham Bzovius.[52] Resuming the work of Cardinal Baronius on the annals of the Church, Bzovius showed by means of numerous references to available sources that he approached the formidable task well prepared. And to Bzovius we owe new evidence for the better knowledge of Wyclyf. Beginning with the imputation to Tauler of the prediction that Wyclyf would rise to lead many people into error,[53] Bzovius added other—and more accurate—observations on the rise of Wyclyf. His chronology is more systematic than that of his predecessors and on the whole corresponds with modern research.[54]

Bzovius was the first to be attracted by Wyclyf's philosophical tenets. He notes Wyclyf's philosophical weapons were forged on the anvil of Democritos and Anaxagoras.[55] It was the latter's view that substance and accident were one the same thing and co-equal with essence which Wyclyf made his own as a young student, and later used in his prime to explain the nature of sacred things.[56] Contending that accidents could not be without subject he came to the point of denying presence of the true and genuine body of Christ in the Holy Eucharist in the form of bread and wine.[57] Bzovius found great satisfaction in pointing out the similarities, if not direct nexus, between the teaching of Wyclyf and recognized heresies of the past, linking him with Arius concerning the futility of prayers for the dead. He connects Vigilantius and Wyclyf in denouncing those Christians as idolaters who honored the saints. Further, Bzovius records that, writing against miracles and the relics of the saints, Wyclyf borrowed his opinions from Eunomius and Vigilantius. He followed the Phariseans and Pelagians in his command to hope in proper justice. Together with Peter Abelard he cast a shadow of doubt on God's omnipotence. When he upheld the notion of absolute necessity which deprived men of free will, he accepted the heresy of the Manicheans, Pelagians, and Predestinatorians. That God did not create all things from nothing was affirmed already by Manes and his disciples.[58] To connect Wyclyf with known heretics was an intellectual exercise on the part of Bzovius which the ordinary reader not in possession of exact information could not verify, and had either to accept or reject at face value. But Bzovius cast aspersions on Wyclyf's renown as a philosopher, citing Wyclyf's vacillating attitude in the matter of the Eucharist, which the Oxford philosopher was never able to solve satisfactorily.[59] Bzovius indicated the contradictions in the terms of "substance" and "figure" which Wyclyf used interchangeably to rationalize the mystery of the Eucharist, and then went on to say: "Moreover, many other things which he had approved in one place he disapproves in another, abandoning the example which he set forth to his followers, that they must be in harmony not only with others, but among themselves."[60] And to convince those who still might not be convinced that Wyclyf was a muddled thinker the keen Dominican added this story which even today is almost always passed over by historians:

> It is said (according to William Woodford) that when at Oxford Wyclyf presented his theses in public and, later, when the responding Bachelor, as they say, he affirmed that the accidents which they call sacramental are in the underlying position: nonetheless the bread remained a substance. But the audience persisted as to what supported those accidents. After long thought he responded: the laws of mathematics.[61]

But it should be noted that Bzovius describes Wyclyf's views on Church property as "Fratricellorum superbissima mendicabula, toties in Conciliis execranda."[62] The fear of the idea of the possible disendowment of the Church was the only one where Catholics and Protestants could meet without rancor and wrath.

It is clear from the preceding selective accounts covering the span of more than two hundred years that at the beginning of the seventeenth century Wyclyf was turning, to repeat the words of John Hus, many a head. His ecclesiastico-political teaching embodied in the *Trialogus* was available in print,[63] and the works of the English fourteenth-century chroniclers were being presented step by step to the reading public.[64] Simultaneously, the revival of learning reintroduced Cicero into the world of the erudites, and no true scholar could afford to neglect the reading of *De oratore* with its apotheosis of history, *lux veritatis* and *magistra vitae*. The examination of sources directly related to Wyclyf's life was undoubtedly stimulated by the humanistic movement and the religious controversy between Catholics and Protestants, but the definition of truth was left in the hands of individual writers. Literature of this period reveals—leaving the question of what is truth unanswered—that the Catholic historians and theologians judged Wyclyf with greater consistency than their Protestant counterparts. For the former he was always a heretic; for the latter, evidence indicates, he was a puzzling personality, if not a "repellent" figure, as Maitland expressed himself on his compatriot.[65] The unalterable position of the Catholics, and the vacillating attitude of the Protestants vis-à-vis Wyclyf, led to the publication of historical appraisals in which moral judgments are the backbone of history.

If we adopt differing judgments of Wyclyf as a yardstick for measuring fundamental differences between the two religious camps, then the Catholics were more agile and certainly more historically minded than the Protestants. Already, before the outbreak of the Thirty Years War and the accession of Louis XIV, France was the bastion of Catholicism, and the printing press together with the *Privilège du Roi* were available to any capable controversialist. In Italy, as well, the papacy commanded respect and nearly unanimous spiritual support. The Protestants were divided, more concerned with day-to-day events than with the resurrection of dead bodies or reputations, however famous they might be. In the Protestant pantheon "the forerunners of the Reformation" were assigned a minor part. There was no place for them in religion where worship was based on direct contact with God, and where no official martyrs were recognized. It seems now that the idea of nationalism would have helped enormously to enhance the prestige of Wyclyf among English Protestants, but with a few exceptions he was never appreciated. Thomas James did write an apology of Wyclyf, to repulse the attacks fulminating from abroad and to allay the distrust attached to his life at home. However, the forty-five condemned articles prevented Wyclyf from becoming a martyr useful to Protestants. They inhibited Protestant believers from enshrining him without misgivings in their hearts, and even though papal excommunication might have been derided in the sixteenth and seventeenth centuries, it still carried weight and stigmatized anybody so attainted. The two religious camps had different beliefs, but their social ideals were identical, and on disendowment and parallel issues the two hostile camps always reconciled their differences, which otherwise drew them so far apart. Wyclyf was a victim of his idealistic views on the connection between property and grace, and to endorse him, it was felt, was to endorse anarchy, and establish in the royal chambers the notorious and ubiquitous: *idiotae, mulierculae,* and other undesirable specimens of the human species. This prospect seemed more horrifying to the scientific seventeenth century than to the superstitious fourteenth century.

It is no exaggeration to say that for the Anglican Church John Wyclyf was an unwelcome historical figure. In 1625 Francis Mason's revised edition of *Vindiciae Ecclesiae Anglicanae,* with a dedication to Thomas James, confuted ten of its detractors ranging from Bellarmin to Stapleton; but nowhere is there any mention of Wyclyf, nowhere is his authority invoked to refute the arguments of Philodoxus, the fictional Catholic personality who exchanges views—like innocent gifts—with Orthodoxus, the Protestant. Mason is in no fighting mood. He even allows Philodoxus to exclaim: "Magna Britannia, dulcissima nostra patria."[66]

Mason was not exceptional but rather indicative of the reaction towards Wyclyf in the seventeenth century. In 1651 Samuel Clarke, answering the demand for popular religious works, published *A Generall Martyrologie*.[67] Clarke started with an eulogy on ecclesiastical history and eventually came to the times of Wyclyf and Hus. He spoke of John Hus and Jerome of Prague in terms of unadulterated adulation (". . . these holy men of God were so unjustly burned at Constance . . . .") but the historian tries in vain to locate the name of John Wyclyf.[68] It is difficult to find the reasons for this omission when Luther was included among the martyrs, and a wreath made of the usually picturesque adjectives adorned his name.[69] Of course, we should not look to him as an authority despite the fulsome praise of the preface:

Away long-winded Volumes, Times disease;
This author doth our phansies better please.
Large Books are endlesse; but 'tis his design
T' enclose great Volumes in his single line.[70]

Seventeenth-century England, however, did not lack occasional vigorous defenders of Wyclyf's memory. One was Thomas Fuller, a preacher and writer, and a prodigious student at Cambridge in his early years, who raised his voice with sympathy and understanding.[71] In 1651 in a book published under one of those titles which are the glory of the seventeenth century, namely *Abel Redevivus,* a collection of worthies, several pages were dedicated to *John Wicklief*.[72] Wyclyf's portrait was based on feelings rather than research. Fuller was the religious Trotsky of the seventeenth century: for him too the revolution was not yet finished. He was sincere when he wrote that after the Oxford condemnation of 1381 [sic]: ". . . all means were used for the suppressing of his [Wyclyf's] opinions; but through God's mercie they could never bee extirpated to this daie."[73] He repeated the stock accusation of the Catholics: "He was a great enemie to the swarms of begging *Friers*."[74] More colorfully and truthfully, he claimed that "the Bishop of *Rome* lost by his Doctrine the power of making and ordaining Bishops in *England,* and the Tenths of spirituall promotions, & also the gains of his *Peter pence*. Whereupon *Polidor Virgil* cals him an infamous Hereticke."[75] This is skillful propaganda combined with denigration wherein Polidore Vergil becomes the real villain. Wyclyf, on the contrary, is styled the "Lampe of England," who, as an unidentified poet says in lesser known verses of the century of Donne:

But, to his death, still, fought faith's fight,
And thus went out this Lamp of Light.[76]

Abel Redevivus was another martyrology, not a historical work. In 1655 Fuller published a more ambitious work, and on this one the fading glow of glory still casts its rays.[77] In the fourth book of this undeniably temperamental work he described the achievements of Wyclyf again, in tones unchanged. He did not use the verses of Ecclesiasticus but the text was saturated with the ponderous adjectives of the seventeenth-century controversialists and apologists. Fuller started with the statement that "I intend neither to deny, dissemble, defend, or excuse any of his faults,"[78] but it is difficult indeed to find a place where Fuller would be truly unhappy with anything that Wyclyf had said. Fuller acknowledged Wyclyf was the product of times when students had to acquire skill ". . . in that abstruse, crabbed divinity, all whose fruit is thornes."[79] He did not believe the stories connecting Wyclyf with Canterbury College and the bishopric of Worcester, and denied that they planted spite in his mind or "incensed him to revenge himself by innovations."[80] And insisting on the moral character of Wyclyf's reform, he formulated a question which was really a *pièce justificative*: "and can true doctrine be the fruit, where ambition and discontent hath been the root thereof?"[81] He surveyed next the varying number of condemned articles from Pope Gregory XI to the publication of Cochlaeus's *Historia Hussitarum* (who increased the count to 303), and concluded delightfully: "The variety ariseth, first, because some count onely his primitive *Tenets*, which are breeders, and others reckon all the yong *frie* of *Consequences* derived from them."[82] Fuller also cited other reasons for this variety, namely, malicious industry and error in authorship. As was fit and proper, Fuller read Netter, and extracted from the latter's *Doctrinale* and *De Sacramentibus* sixty-two articles which in the eyes of the *athleta dei* of the fifteenth century were heretical.[83] But Fuller did not find them such, which in a Protestant, was fair enough, nor did he find them detrimental to Protestant faith which, coming from a Protestant, sounded like a platitude but in fact was not. Fuller finds ". . . an overplus of his [Wyclyf's] passion . . ." in many of them but also admits final judgment should be reserved when so many of Wyclyf's texts were still wanting.[84] Nor was he certain what Wyclyf really meant: all the "limitations, restrictions, distinctions, qualifications" Wyclyf might have inserted were not available.[85] Despite the mentioned reservations Fuller was convinced that "some of his poysonous passages, dres'd with due caution, would prove not onely wholsome, but cordial truths."[86] Although his books masquerade as history, the conclusion is inevitable that Fuller was not a historian. He did not insist on truth and objectivity: he wanted examples. This significant trait, common to all the moralists, is exemplified in the electrical and nervous scene of the St. Paul's hearing. For the first time since Foxe the drama was reprinted in full, word by word. Wyclyf, writes Fuller, there "made but a dumb shew."[87] Before abandoning Wyclyf, Fuller cleared his subject of any possible association with the rebels—"rabble of rebels"—of 1381, enumerating eight reasons for rejecting the charges made by "ingenuous papists," and suggested that the rebellion started from a Franciscan convent.[88] With an affirmation that Wyclyf was witness of the truth, he passes on to Wickham, his orchard of grown trees and his nursery of grafts in Winchester.[89]

Roger Twysden was a writer of a different mold. Whereas Fuller indulged in what could be called the tropical heat of verbal argument—and his command of the English language supplied him generously with the necessary fuel—the former preferred to conceal himself behind arguments in which words were of lesser importance than the issue they represented. In *An Historical Vindication of the Church of England in Point of Schism* Twysden appropriated a more genuine historical method as the vehicle for elucidation of an issue which has haunted the Church of England from the moment of its royal inception; defending the existence of an independent royal policy toward the Church of Rome, he relied on Wyclyf's *Responsio* of 1377, which sustained the royal prerogative in financial and fiscal matters of the realm to the exclusion of all other rights. (Twysden was not as well informed as to what stimulated the *Responsio,* since he spoke in this connection of Peter's Pence).[90] Wyclyf was drawn into the same argument once more when Twysden expressed doubts whether the decisions of the Fourth Lateran Council on transubstantiation were ever accepted in England. Discussing this intriguing problem, he suggested that Wyclyf started to propound *quod substantia panis materialis aut vini manet post consecrationem* in 1377, and hastily added: "But this is a point rather dogmatical for divines, than historical—the subject by me undertaken—I shall not here farther wade into."[91] Twysden's method surely was historical, if not too historical. The quotation above indicates that Twysden contemplated theological problems only when he was forced by circumstances to do so, and thus it is difficult to know what he thought of Wyclyf. Handling all the historical personalities in his books like emotionless chess figures on the checker-board of history, Twysden faces us like a chess figure himself.

In 1685 it was still possible to write a history of a reign and leave out the protagonist of the scene without whom the rest of the play was a display of nonsense. Sir Robert Howard, who undertook to review *The History of the Reigns of Edward and Richard II; with reflections, and characters of their chief ministers and favourites,* chose a title to which he remained unfaithful without any scruples. We may safely assume he spoke for many a contemporary of Leibnitz, Descartes, and Newton when he characterized the problems of the scholastic philosophers as "Subtil Nothings" or "brangling—cobweb—Controversies," but the then anticipated tirade against Wyclyf never appears.[92] He was eliminated—by what reasoning we do not know—from the narrative, although Howard does treat the duke of Lancaster and the "mass of giddiness" (by which were meant the rising of 1381).[93]

Joshua Barnes's *Victorious King Edward III* is richly embroidered with the thread of military campaigns.[94] The ghost of Froissart always hovers protectingly above the lines as Barnes, eschewing judgment or comment, trumpeted the monotonous regularity of battle and victory, victory and battle.[95] However, there is a passage in Barnes which was not in Froissart. We know that for some unknown reason Froissart never mentioned Wyclyf, so that Barnes used a different source to integrate Wyclyf into the story. With the help of Anthony à Wood, he knew more about Wyclyf's Oxford life than anybody before him, and by 1688 Merton, Balliol, and Canterbury Hall were firmly associated with the Wyclyf tradition.[96] Barnes was careful to say that Wyclyf "is supposed to have Translated the Old and New Testament into English" but he was wrong when he added "from the Original Hebrew and Greek."[97] And, he adds, all was done "with no bad Design, as we may presume."[98] He correctly dates the first hearing with the bishops in St. Paul's Cathedral on 19 February 1377, and, with a sense for understatement, not very common in those times, he reminds the reader that Wyclyf "affirm'd sundry Doctrines very disagreeable to the Genius of that Age."[99] Barnes's account has its refreshing moments, as when he appeals to "Honest Knighton,"[100] but otherwise it strangely prefigured the dry and stereotyped accounts of the nineteenth century, written for information without inspiration.

Another historian who touched upon Wyclyf was Gilbert Burnet, bishop of Salisbury, the "man of war since his youth." John Wyclyf was not for him a *causa belli* against the world, nor were Wyclyf's opponents in the world of controversy in which Burnet moved with undeniable agility and gusto. In his *History of the Reformation* Burnet provided space for Wyclyf, but the way in which he did it left no doubt that he was interested in Wyclyf only as a nuisance which could not be overlooked. He repeated the stock categories: Bible, images, real presence, and avoided personal judgments. He preferred to refer to the uncertainty as to what Wyclyf really said and even his opinion concerning the translation of the Bible is not clear.[101] At any rate Burnet did not feel happy about Wyclyf's followers who were more impressed with the Bible and its preface through common sense and plain reason than deep speculation or study; they were furthermore illiterate and ignorant men.[102] Moreover, Burnet designates Thomas Fuller, one of the few Anglican clerics at that time in favor of Wyclyf, as "a man of fancy," "affecting an odd way of writing," whose "work gives no great satisfaction."[103] John Milton characterized Bishop Burnet and all those who followed him by saying that theirs was "a devotion [which] comes to that queazy temper of luke-warmnesse, that gives a Vomit to God himselfe . . . ."[104]

However, it was not the book of the bishop of Salisbury which gave impulse to the memorable debate of the 1680's, but a tiny volume by Antoine Varillas, a historian more by title than by achievement. In 1682 he embarked on an enterprise which took him on very stormy seas to disaster. He decided to write a history of "Wiclefianisme," that is to say the doctrine of Wyclyf, John Hus, and Jerome of Prague, and the motive is disclosed in the *Avertissement*.[105] The author felt, said the anonymous writer of the preface, that the history of the Lutheran and Calvinist heresies was incomplete without "une connoissance un peu exacte" of the heresies of Wyclyf, Hus, and Jerome.[106]

It is impossible to indicate all the gross and picayune mistakes that Varillas managed to insert into his work. Some are undeniably part of the intent of the writer to dramatize daily life, and romanticize history with undocumented but always effective blows of God. Some are the result of carelessness which could have been avoided even in the seventeenth century. Thus Varillas makes Wyclyf Regius Professor at Oxford—a title and position created in the reign of Henry VIII.[107] Varillas described Wyclyf as a master dissembler, a conspirator waiting in silence for the proper moment, reading in the meantime all the schismatic works defending emperors and antipopes against the papacy. Wyclyf, rails Varillas, was in touch with the feelings of the most recent heretics, extracting knowledge from those poisoned sources which could more easily be "insinuées aux Anglois, parce qu'elles avoient plus de rapport avec leur génie."[108] By changing the name of Alice Perrers to Aliz Perez, he had no difficulty thereafter in identifying her as "une Espagnolle."[109] Moreover, he makes the royal mistress a powerful supporter of Wyclyf, whose eloquence and extraordinary merit she, together with the duke of Lancaster, continually extolled to the king. The association of the duke with Wyclyf, according to our author, was the result of the aspirations of the duke to the English throne and the desire of Wyclyf to have a propertyless clergy. The duke needed someone, first to spread his fame and minimize the renown of the Black Prince, and secondly to attach the people to his person—without any obvious effort on his part. In this scheme invented by Varillas, Wyclyf presumably helped Lancaster through his demand for confiscation of Church estates. On the political plane Varillas concludes, the plan would have meant loss of the barons's power in Parliament and the victory of the Commons. And the Commons, because of the popularity of Wyclyf's teaching, then would have supported Lancaster, and above all his claim to the throne. On the other hand Lancaster would have sacrificed the political status of the barons and the clergy to Wyclyf as a reward for his support and work on Lancaster's behalf among the townspeople.[110] This is a typical illustration of Varillas's interpretative genius and unrelieved ignorance. The book is a continuous historical romance. It is difficult to decide whether one is reading the work of a fabricator of a legend, or the precursor of *Wahreheit und Dichtung,* or the horror paperback.[111] We do not know whether he was a historian in love with his subject, or a professional sycophant, or one molded by circumstances and financial opportunities.

In 1685 Louis XIV decided to abrogate the legal religious tolerance which existed since Henry IV's promulgation of the Edict of Nantes. One aspect of the revocation cannot escape the attention of the Wyclyf historian. It induced M. Varillas to write a more ambitious work than the *Wiclefianisme* on the existence of the reformed religions in Europe: the *Histoire des Révolutions arrivées dans l'Europe en matiére de Religion,* dedicated to Louis XIV in these words: "L'Histoire des dernieres Révolutions arrivées dans l'Europe en matiere de Religion, contient un si bel endroit pour le Panegirique de VOSTRE MAJESTE, qu'il y auroit de l'ignorance ou de la malice à le supprimer."[112]

Setting, significantly, his *terminus a quo* in 1374, he could not brush aside Wyclyf. The account of Wyclyf in the *Histoire* was an enlarged version of the fable which we have examined previously. The old injuries he had inflicted on the history of Wyclyf were reopened. Wat Tyler's name, according to Varillas, was Gauthier Igler.[113] Wyclyf "se retira dans la Province de Galles nouvellement assujettie aux Anglois, où il s'insinua dans l'esprit du peuple en flattant ses deux passions dominantes, qui consistoient dans une aversion irreconciliable pour l'Ordre de saint Benoist & dans un mépris extraordinaire de Clergé."[114] However, we are treated to the correct date of his death. Somewhere (was it in Stow?) he discovered that it was 31 December 1384.[115] This time Varillas's book did not escape censure: from England he was obliged to hear the unfriendly critique of Burnet, who did not object particularly to what Varillas had to say on Wyclyf, but who was irritated by what the Frenchman offered on the English Reformation, the undisputed domain of the pugnacious Anglican bishop.

Gilbert Burnet did not spare the French historian. He attacked his latest work as the "falsest coyn that can be struck."[116] He let Varillas know that his own compatriots told Burnet that "the greatest number of the pieces he cited were to be found no where but in his own fancy."[117] He lectured Varillas on the meaning of history several times with the tone of one who knew what history was.[118] He reminded Varillas that he "did not find any Man under a more universal Contempt than he was,"[119] and prophesied that "he will very probably soon lose his appointments, since mercenary Pens are seldom payed longer than they can be useful."[120] Burnet reproached Varillas his errors and then crowned the polemic with the ironic sigh, ". . . but he finds out new matter to write on, and a new stock of *Champaigne* wine, as I have been told, that he has oft said, to make his blood boyl till he has spoil'd another piece of History; . . . ."[121] Burnet addressed fifty-two objections to Varillas, the first also related to our matters. Burnet objected to the assertion made by Varillas that Wyclyf's heresy was so entirely rooted out in England that during the reign of Henry VII the whole nation was of the same religion. Burnet reminded him that in 1511 there were forty-one processes instituted against "certain persons" in the registers of the see of Canterbury.[122] (He did not say whether they were Wyclyfites or Lollards or some other heretics.) He admitted moreover that "the Opinions, objected to those Persons, shew, that the Reformation found a disposition in the nation, to receive it by the Doctrines which were entertained by many in it: For the chief of them are . . .": the "Sacrament of the Altar was not Christ's Body," image worship, pilgrimages, and prayers to saints.[123] (There was again no mention of Wyclyf.)

Varillas answered the critical observations of Burnet by another *résponse*, dedicated to his king.[124] He replied to every objection raised by Burnet. In the first place he analyzed the words "those Persons," a term he translated as *prétendus Hérétiques*, and suggested they meant the Wyclyfites, thus putting into the mouth of Burnet a word the latter tried to avoid so studiously.[125] Burnet again replied to the objections but without any enthusiasm. He dismissed Varillas's argument concerning the Wyclyfites in a cavalier way, and ended the debate.[126] This was, however, only the beginning of the protracted controversy on the merits of Wyclyf in the declining years of the seventeenth century.[127]

The literary battle between M. Varillas and Mr. Burnet was but a
skirmish with the lightest arms in comparison with the massive salvo
of historical *non sequiturs* fired on the persecuted Varillas by Daniel
de Larroque. In Larroque Wyclyf studies received, in 1687, the first
scholar worthy of the name, and if his slender work had been used
more profusely after its publication it would have saved many an author from future mistakes. Larroque was a destroyer of Varillas's
myths. He could not escape the temptation of dealing several times in
lighter vein with the most flagrant of Varillas's inaccuracies, such as
the spelling of *Enthelrod* and *Lutzorod* for *Lutterworth,* but for the
most part he studied the text of Varillas with the help of the published
works of Walsingham, Knighton, the author of *Polichronicon,* Spel-
man, Anthony à Wood, Harpsfield, Polydore Vergil, Labbé, Bzovius,
and Bale.[128] It seems that there was not a source he had not covered,
and covered well, retaining in his mind not only the discrepancies
existing between Varillas and the sources, but also among the texts
themselves. He was thus able to bring into his account—still fresh
today after three hundred years—the affair of Canterbury College;[129]
and he established the date of Wyclyf's attack on transubstantiation as between 1377 and 1381 by showing that the papal bulls of 1377
were silent on the Sacrament of the Altar.[130] He broke on the wheel
of remorseless logic and knowledge the fantasy of Varillas concerning
the triangle of the duke of Lancaster, Alice Perrers, and Wyclyf,[131] and
he was probably the first to put down that Wyclyf's name was submitted for correction to Pope Gregory XI by the monks, "plûtôt par
un esprit de calomnie que par amour pour la verité."[132] Larroque did
not avoid the pitfalls of the Wyclyf studies—the dates of Wyclyf's
trials—and chastised Varillas for statements which the latter had ba-
sically correct even though he did not fully understand their intrinsic
and textual connection.[133] The realization that there were two prosecutions, one in 1377 and the other in 1378, gained ground very slowly.
David Wilkins had not yet started work on the *Concilia,* and Walsingham, as Larroque indicated, was not an accurate recorder though "pour
un Moine du quinzième siécle est pourtant un assez habile homme."[134]
With evident relish Larroque mistrusted the alleged union between
Wyclyf and John Ball, and dismissed the fabricated interpretation that
Wyclyf was a party leader.[135] He accepted (was it for the first time?)
a statement concerning the abjuration of Wyclyf borrowed from Knighton and preached this short moral sermon, which is not without irony:
"Tous les Historiens en conveniennent, & insultent avec raison à la
lâchete de ce Docteur, qui après avoir fait mille fanfaronnades, comme
ces faux braves qui n'ont de courage qu'éloignez du péril, se rétracta

de la manière la plus basse qu'on puisse imaginer."[136] (In twenty-seven years after many peregrinations in divers countries of Europe Larroque gave up his Protestant conviction, adopted the old faith and acquired a comfortable post in the bureaucracy.)

Larroque viewed Wyclyf with the understanding "qu'il avoit toutes les qualitez de l'esprit propres à faire un grand homme quand il naît dans un Siécle heureux."[137] For a man of the fourteenth century he knew the Scriptures sufficiently well ("passablement").[138] He was a lion who was feared while alive but was insulted as soon as he died, a result of a common cowardice of "Messieurs les Auteurs" who have most of the time more intellectual than moral virtues. Never was Posterity more unjust than with respect to his "Sçavant Homme."[139] Larroque knew that certain Protestant writers wanted to make Wyclyf even more orthodox than Calvin, and he cited Thomas James, whom Larroque recognized as a scholar and characterized as a violent man, only to dismiss his *Apology* as a vain work.[140]

Larroque did not believe in the genuineness of the forty-five condemned articles. On the other hand he ascribed the Lollard composition *Wyclif's Wicket* to Wyclyf. Larroque also raised the issue of Wyclyf's interpretation of the Scriptures, claiming he gave them meaning "bien differens de ceux qu'on lui doit donner."[141] As a person, Wyclyf was presumptuous, says the Frenchman, and did not possess the qualities of a leader; he had an unbalanced character, and lacked "la delicatesse de conscience qu'un véritable Chrêtien doit avoir."[142] Larroque then pronounces his final judgment: ". . . il avoit plûtôt les sentimens d'un Quaker & d'un indépendent, que d'un Protestant ou d'un Catholique."[143]

All this complicated discussion which started so innocuously in Lyon in 1682, and developed subsequently into a regular war between the opponents and supporters of Wyclyf, was joined in England in 1688 by William King, whose "Language and Expression" unfortunately were indeed "without Choice and Ornament."[144] Although we know so little about him in the realm of facts, King was, as far as the *Advertisement* discloses, a prig and a snob. He assured the reader in one sentence that he ought to take part in the exposure of Varillas "in the part concerning Wicliff, having formerly laid together some observations conducing to such a design"; in the next sentence, however, the text revealed his true feelings in these jingoistic terms: "Mr. L'arroque [*sic*] indeed has gone before him in the attempt; but that ingenious Gentleman was not well advis'd to meddle in a strange Countrey, till time had instructed him more fully in the Constitutions and Language of it."[145] In the body of the booklet all the arguments, facts and criticisms assembled by Larroque were fully exploited. There is not one single contribution in the text which deserves to be called original. What was new were the judgments, the moral beating of the Protestant breast, the affected wisdom of an half-empty brain. We must be grateful, however, to William King for this book which was, in fact and in an odd way, a defence of Wyclyf against the accumulated inaccuracies of the centuries. It is refreshing to read after the aridly monotonous condemnations of Wyclyf as a rabble-rouser, for in King's independent view, "*Wicliff's* Preaching had no more relation to this Rebellion, than the Edition of *Confucius* in *France* had to the Sufferings of the *Hugonots,* or than Mr. *Varillas's Conclusions* are us'd to have to his Premises."[146] New social criteria of the seventeenth century came into full view when King exculpated Wyclyf from the odious charge of being a disseminator of dissension by noting that "he himself took his *Degree of Doctor.*"[147]

In the same year the speaking conscience of France, Jacques-Bénigne Bossuet, bishop of Meaux, entered the literary fray with a work which summed up the Catholic doctrine against the Protestants, and marked the end of the controversy which since 1520 had flourished in Europe regardless of political atmosphere. The *Histoire des variations des Églises protestantes,* certainly stimulated by contemporary literature, aimed not only at his own times, but also was intended as a legacy to future generations. Bossuet was in many parts of his work replying to Burnet. It would be a mistake not to see that below the veneer of the seventeenth-century literary conventions there lay the thought that Bossuet considered the Reformation as a disobedience of passing duration. On the other hand he was not unaware of the claims of some Protestants who, in an endeavor to establish harmony with fifteen hundred years of Christianity, were forced at last to identify their own saints and confessors. Book XI of the *Histoire des variations* inserted (it seems, as an afterthought) the Albigensians, Valdensians, Wyclyfites and the Hussites, but left out, mainly for practical reasons, all the fragmentary sects. (Bossuet nevertheless was aware of them.) The first sentence sounds a trumpet call to rally the available forces: "Ce qu'ont entrepris nos Reformez, pour se donner des predecesseurs dans tous les siecles passes est inouï."[148] He classifies Wyclyf among them as a Protestant predecessor *de iure.*

Bossuet is an exegesist who goes to the sources, and then declares them invalid for the Catholic Christian. He approached Wyclyf with a thorough knowledge of Wyclyf's *Trialogus* which was, he wants us to believe, "ce livre fameux qui souleva toute la Boheme, & excita tant de troubles en Angleterre."[149] He gave the first lengthy summary of the text, being most startled by Wyclyf's notion of divine necessity. Bossuet's analysis deserves to be quoted in full:

> Voilà un extrait fidéle de ses blasphêmes: ils se reduisent à deux chefs, à faire un Dieu dominé par la necessité, & ce qui en est une suite, un Dieu auteur & approbateur de tous les crimes, c'est-à-dire, un Dieu que les Athées auroient raison de nier, de sorte que la Religion d'un si grand reformateur est pire que l'athéisme.[150]

Bossuet then infers that Luther followed Wyclyf, and, not without reason, that the Calvinists had reckoned him—"cet impie"—among their predecessors.[151] The bishop of Meaux, still following the text of the *Trialogus*, came then to the delicate problems of Church property, and the possibility of secular interference in Church matters. Bossuet's comment is forthright: "Me permettra-t-on de le dire? Voilà dans un Anglois le premier modele de la reformation Anglicane & de la depredation des Eglises."[152]

It is at this stage of the narrative that the bishop, beginning to feel the heat of the issue, casts aside his philosophical cloak, to take up the weapons of the polemicist. His chief target was Larroque. Bossuet questioned the claim of Larroque that article 6, *Deus debet obedire diabolo,* was surreptitiously introduced by the Council of Constance, and ended up with the same argument as Gretser: "Mais si nous trouvons tant de blasphêmes dans un seul ouvrage qui nous reste de Wiclef, on peut bien croire qu'il y en avoit beaucoup d'autres dans les livres qu'on avoit alors en si grand nombre; . . . ."[153] Furthermore, the belief in article 6 was the result of the doctrine of divine necessity: God was bound by necessity to do certain things—among others, to follow the will of the Devil.[154] And to prove that Wyclyf was not always acceptable even to the Protestants, Bossuet quoted Melanchthon on Wyclyf, presenting a picture of the humanist which since then has always been useful for all those who were opposed to the idea that Wyclyf belonged to the early Protestant prophets.[155]

Europe had reached a point of no return by 1688 as far as religion was concerned. The religious unity Bossuet so ardently desired was unattainable. The reaction of Bishop Burnet, who never missed the opportunity to confute Catholic pronouncements, was characteristic, and dispelled any hopes of a coming reunion of (in the words of Bossuet) Israel and Judah. Burnet acknowledges great respect for Bossuet's age and character but repudiates Bossuet's proffer of reunion in these words: "If all was not at first discovered, the Changes that the Reformers made, was a Progress and not a Variation."[156] And he

dismissed the work, "writ to as little purpose as can be," with the
complaisant advice: "A Man of his Wit and Softness of Expression,
should have held himself to general Speculations, in which a lively
Fancy and a good Stile, might have helped him out even when Truth
failed him."[157] As a note of interest, let it be added that in his *Censure*,
Burnet did not defend Wyclyf.

There was little hope for change. The states were assuming their
modern appearance, and the minds of their people, shaped as they
were at the end of the seventeenth century in a climate imbued with
Protestantism in all its facets, were not receptive to ideas of another
radical departure. When in 1694 Henrich [*sic*] Ludolff Benthem published his *Engländischer Kirch- und Schulen-Staat,* a prototype of the
later Baedecker guides, he was able to report on English life in pictures
which remained unchanged for many generations. He spoke of the
English as having thick air and clouded skies but subtle and keen
minds. He characterized the English language as *Mischmasch.* He
described the scene in Hyde Park where ordinary street coaches were
not allowed to enter. He knew that an interested person could visit the
library of the archbishop of Canterbury if he was on good terms with
its librarian, and he did not fail to mention that youngsters played ball
in the streets during the winter months to keep warm. He drew attention to the great English holidays, Guy Fawkes Day, and the commemoration of Queen Elizabeth on November 17, and described how
on those days the pope was burnt in effigy in front of Temple Bar.[158]

As a good travel guide for students, which was the book's primary
purpose, it included a historical description of Oxford, and Benthem
spoke of the former, great masters who taught there. One of them was
"der bekannte Johannes Wiclef, Sacrae paginae Professor, welcher
1387, gestorben."[159] Benthem was not historically minded, but an observer with an inquisitive mind from whom we grasp to what extent
Wyclyf's memory was interesting outside of theological controversy.
We learn that sometime between 1683 and 1686, when he was in England, there was in St. John's College a Bible translated and written by
Wyclyf, which could be seen on request. As a well-informed traveller,
he adds that in many places it differed from the existing English version.[160] The feeling is inescapable, reading this account of Benthem
nowadays, that at the end of the seventeenth century England had
almost completely left medieval notions behind on its way toward a
new period already instinctively felt but yet unknown, and perhaps
unimaginable. In this new world Bishop Bossuet spoke a language
already incomprehensible to the scholar and of no consequence to the
people at large.

If we survey the course of the seventeenth century and measure the importance attached to John Wyclyf by the writers of this period, we come to the conclusion that among the historians and theologians who tried to interpret the present with the help of the past, the willingness to extoll Wyclyf was more than counterbalanced by the reluctance to accept him as a *bona fide* Protestant. The complex figure of Wyclyf, whom many viewed darkly through the glass of the forty-five condemned articles, defied an easy, standard classification. Even those who tried to be sympathetic had to wrestle with their consciences, social and religious allegiances, and vested interests before they embraced him without a Judas-like kiss. We have witnessed the performances of Thomas James and Thomas Fuller in the field of Wyclyf apologetics, and the number could be easily increased by the lesser lights who reflected the bright rays of the intellectual planets.

Richard Baxter, a "hater of false History," wrote for those "who cannot read many and great Volumes," and was caught in the same dilemma.[161] When he came to the notorious article 6 he did not comment on it at all but simply said in the margin: "A calumny."[162] When he approached article 17 (that the people could correct their delinquent lords) he assumed the customary position: "This is not to be believed to be Wickliff's sense, till they cite his own words, which no doubt limit it to the cases."[163] It is permissible to doubt Baxter's knowledge of Wyclyf's works and it is permissible to doubt Baxter's respect for truth when he asserts: "This Article about *Necessity of Events,* I see in *Wickliff's* Books is his own, and many here cited are true; but no doubt but many of them are perverted by their wording them, and leaving out the Explicatory Context."[164] It would be unjust to claim that in the seventeenth century there was no enthusiasm for Wyclyf and his work. But unlike the medieval pilgrimage which brought solace and entertainment, the pilgrimage to the fount of Wyclyf's views ended often in discomfiture and perplexity.

If we look across the countries of Western Europe to the kingdom of Bohemia and its university, where Wyclyf's ideas received their home after they had been proscribed and banished from the surface of the universe, even there the seventeenth century was not the proper time for the veneration or even remembrance of someone who bore the stigma of a heresiarch. Between 1618–1648, during the somber period of the Thirty Years War, daily politics occupied the minds of men more than the past. The clash of religious beliefs which occurred in 1609, whose repercussions were drowned in the murmur of the drums around the gallows and ended with the blow of the executioner's sword in 1619, turned the Thirty Years War, at least for the Czechs, into a religious struggle, and made religious liberty its main issue. The peace of Münster and Osnabrück put the seal of defeat and beginning despair on the non-Catholic inhabitants; in an Exodus which lacked the vision of a promised land they left the country where their birth rights were invalidated by their firm faith.

Jan Amos Komenský (Comenius), spiritual leader of the exiles, was left in the last years of his life without hope of returning to his country. Rationalizing the course of his life, he brought comfort to his trials and to those dispersed in the many countries of Europe through books designed to interpret the past and place hope in the future. Komenský spoke of Wyclyf in the *Haggaeus Redivivus,* where he classed him with other reformers—Luther, Calvin, Zwingli. In a composition which sounds like a sorrowful prayer he thinks of him as a tool of God.[165] However, in his most moving work, the farewell message to his nation and the Bohemian Church, he exhorted his nation to love God's truth which "was shown for the first time by Master John Hus through the grace of the Lord."[166]

In the second half of the seventeenth century the outstanding Czech Jesuit Bohuslav Balbin in the *Epitome historica rerum bohemicarum* briefly mentions Wyclyf only when he approaches the transmission of Wyclyfite ideas to Bohemia; and his information is drawn from Hajek of Libocan, who tried, in an imaginery dialogue between the two condemned heretics, to alleviate the guilt which after 1415 became inexcusable.[167] Balbin was a patriot just like Komenský, but he stood on the other side of the Christian frontier. It is not surprising that Balbin's most profound treatise is a *Defence of the Czech language* written just at the time it was a disgrace to speak it.[168] The seventeenth century in Bohemia was primarily, as Ernest Denis correctly stated, *La fin de l'indépendance.*[169] Both Komenský and Balbin realized very well that the new period under the Habsburgs was threatening the life of the nation. The people could survive, they insisted, only by maintaining their language, loving each other, and hoping. This was their legacy formulated at a time when "kingdoms were passing away and many were changing their forms including their nations, languages, laws and religions, because without any doubts a new age was being ushered in."[170] Under these circumstances it was vain, especially in Balbin's times, to foment disturbances in religious matters while the nation was agonizing.

Against the deliberate ambiguity of the seventeenth-century men hitherto considered, we may set at least one writer—not a historian, not a theologian, but an unsuppressed believer in the regeneration of the Church—who declared himself for Wyclyf in straightforward prose. John Milton was opposed to hierarchy, and to the dazzling heights of the episcopal see, and he had the courage to say it. When he wrote *Of Reformation Touching Church-Discipline in England,* he expressed his conviction that ". . . it is still *Episcopacie* that before all our eyes worsens and sluggs the most learned, and seeming religious of our *Ministers* . . . ,"[171] and accused the bishops of "belching the Soure Crudities of yesterdayes *Poperie* . . . ."[172] He recognized the value which again money had acquired in recent times, and, deeply upset, he could not but warn that "if the splendor of *Gold* and *Silver* begin to Lord it once againe in the Church of *England,* wee shall see *Antichrist* shortly wallow heere, though his cheife Kennell be at *Rome.*"[173] Milton shared with Wyclyf the horror of seeing the Church defiled, God adjured, and worship debased by human inventions and human minds assuming the position of God himself. Milton identified the Church of Rome of the past as the Corrupt Church, convinced that it was only redeemed with the arrival of the Reformation. He accepted, however, precursors of the Reformation, and he also believed that England (the "Lost Darling" of the papists) was God's land where His will and mercy had to descend first.[174] And he lent to this belief the beauty of his words, and the ringing confidence of a religious man who still believed wholeheartedly: If God was with us who was against us? The lengthy passage in which he connected all these thoughts with Wyclyf deserves to be quoted in full:

> . . . let us recount even here without delay the patience and long suffering that God hath us'd towards our blindnesse and hardness time after time. For he being equally neere to his whole Creation of Mankind, and of free power to turne his benefick and fatherly regard to what Region or Kingdome he pleases, hath yet ever had this Iland under the speciall indulgent eye of his providence; and pittying us the first of all other Nations, after he had decreed to purifie and renew his Church that lay wallowing in Idolatrous pollutions, sent first to us a healing messenger to touch softly our sores, and carry a gentle hand over our wounds: he knockt once and twice and came againe, opening our drousie eye-lids leasurely by that glimmering light which *Wicklef,* and his followers dispers't, and still taking off by degrees the inveterat scales from our nigh perisht sight, purg'd also our deaf eares, and prepar'd them to attend his second warning trumpet in our Grandsires dayes. How else could they have beene able to have receiv'd the sudden assault of his reforming Spirit warring against humane Principles, and carnall sense, the pride of flesh that still cry'd up Antiquity, Custome, Canons, Councels and Lawes, and cry'd down the truth for noveltie, schisme, profanenesse and sacriledge: when as we that have liv'd so long in abundant light, besides the sunny reflection of all the neighbouriug [sic] Churches, have yet our hearts rivetted with those old opinions, and so obstructed and benumm'd with the same fleshly reasonings, which in our forefathers soone melted and gave way, against the morning beam of *Reformation.*[175]

Three years later, in the most memorable speech ever pronounced on the liberty of expression, Milton turned again to Wyclyf, to England, and the Reformation. In ringing prose he proclaimed:

> Why else was this Nation chos'n before any other, that out of her as out of *Sion* should be proclam'd and sounded forth the first tidings and trumpet of Reformation to all *Europ*. And had it not bin the obstinat perversnes of our Prelats against the divine and admirable spirit of Wicklef, to suppresse him as a schismatic and *innovator,* perhaps neither the *Bohemian Husse* and *Jerom,* no nor the name of *Luther,* or of *Calvin* had bin ever known: the glory of reforming all our neighbours had bin compleatly ours.[176]

Such religious and national pride blended to what amounts to Protestant mysticism was not, as I have tried to show, shared by other English divines and writers of that period. But the voice of Milton was long remembered, for in the nineteenth century Macaulay used nearly the same words to greet the memory of that "divine and admirable spirit."[177]

Notes

[1] Nicholas Vignier, *Recueil de l'histoire de l'Église, depuis le Baptesme de Notre Seigneur Jésus-Christ, iusques à ce temps* (Leyden, 1601).

[2] *Ibid.,* p. 556.

[3] *Ibid.,* p. 558.

[4] *Ibid.,* p. 557.

[5] Disputationum Roberti Bellarmini Politiani, S. R. E. Cardinalis, Tit. S. Mariae in Via, *De Controversiis christianae fidei, adversus huius temporis haereticos,* rev. ed., 4 vols. (Ingolstadt, 1601).

[6] Already at the end of the sixteenth century Netter's *Doctrinale* was available in three editions: Paris, 1532; Salamanca, 1556–7; and Venice, 1571.

[7] *Ibid.,* II, col. 617. Bellarmin expounded the views of Archbishop Fitzralph on the poverty of Christ and finished by saying, "Haec omnia sunt contra apertas Scripturas, ..." *Ibid.,* II, col. 618.

[8] Bellarmin used the same approach when he discussed various sentences by writers of the past on the nature of Christ's body in the Eucharist. *Ibid.,* III, col. 713.

[9] "Primum enim quaeremus, an potuerit Deus reipsa praesens exhibere corpus & sanguinem Domini in specie panis & vini. Deinde an voluerit.

"De prima quaestione Ioannes Wiclefus apud Thomam Waldensem, tom. 2. cap. 72. & 73. & eius discipulus Ioannes Calvinus aperte negant id posse fieri." *Ibid.,* III, col. 658.

[10] "Rupertus igitur docuit, panem Eucharistiae hypostatice assumi a Verbo, eo prorsus modo, quo natura humana ab eodem Verbo assumpta est . . . . Idem auctor in 2. libro de divinis officiis, cap. 2. fuse idipsum docet: ubi declarat ipsum panem fieri corpus Christi, non quia vertatur in carnem Domini, sed quia assumatur a Verbo. Ex quo sequitur panem esse corpus Christi, sed corpus non humanum, neque carneum, sed panaceum; & longe diversum ab illo, quod de Virgine sumptum est. Ibidem docet, haec duo corpora posse dici unum, quia unum est suppositum utriusque, sive unus est Christus, qui utrumque assumpsit: & disertis verbis dicit, illa corpora, panaceum, & carneum, esse unum, quia idem Christus sursum, id est, in coelo, est in carne, deorsum, id est, in altari, est in pane." *Ibid.,* III, cols. 712–13.

[11] Thomas James, *An Apologie for Iohn Wickliffe, . . .* (Oxford, 1608), p. 20.

[12] *Ibid.*, pp. 19, 30.

[13] For Oxford University Wyclyf was still in 1530 "apostolus tam impudens quam temerarius" who "superseminavit zizania in medio tritici et boni seminis." British Library, Lansdowne MS. 446, fol. 63 r.

[14] James, *Apologie*, Preface, p. 1.

[15] *Ibid.*, p. 14.

[16] *Ibid.*, pp. 33, 37. [By the Bald Priest he means John Ball.]

[17] *Ibid.*, p. 42.

[18] *Ibid.*, p. 64.

[19] *Ibid.*, pp. 58–60.

[20] James also mentions *Liber de blasphemia* and *Expositio Decalogi.*

[21] *Ibid.*, sign. K 3 r.

[22] *Ibid.*, sign. K 3 v.

[23] *Ibid.*, sign. K (4) v.

[24] James went as far as to accuse the Jesuits of using "goodly paper, faire letters, and glorious annotations, whereby they have bewitched the whole world . . . ." *Ibid.*, p. 73.

[25] *Ibid.*, p. 20.

[26] Bellarmin never used colorful adjectives and never indulged in name-calling. Gretser called James "crassissimus sycophanta et calumniator" and characterized Luther's teaching as "mendacium luculentum." Jacob Gretser, *Controversiam Roberti Bellarmini S. R. E. Cardinalis Amplissimi Defensio*, 2 vols. (Ingolstadt, 1607–9), I, cols. 1061, 2047.

[27] *Ibid.*, I, 8.

[28] *Idem.*

[29] *Ibid.*, I, 9.

[30] *Idem.*

[31] *Ibid.*, I, 25.

[32] *Ibid.*, I, 831.

[33] *Idem.*

[34] Melchior Cano, "De locis theologicis libri duodecim," *Opera* (Coloniae Agrippinae, 1605), pp. 1–739.

[35] *Ibid.*, p. 191.

[36] *Ibid.*, p. 195.

[37] *Ibid.*, p. 378.

[38] *Ibid.*, p. 414.

[39] "Homines enim ab humanis affectibus alieni esse non possumus. Hinc est quod licet propter praesentis temporis iniquitatem, maiorem vitae meae partem in exteris regionibus exul egerim, non possum tamen oblivisci patriae in qua natus sum, parentum & maiorum a quibus procreatus sum, & eorum omnium quorum rerum gestarum gloria semper futura est omni posteritati virtutis calcar & incitamentum." John Pits, *Relationum Historicarum de Rebus Anglicis Tomus Primus* . . . (Paris, 1619), p. 1. The work is better known under its secondary title *De illustribus Angliae Scriptoribus.*

[40] *Ibid.*, Dedication, p. 8.

[41] *Ibid.*, p. 52.

[42] *Ibid.*, p. 53.

[43] *Idem.*

[44] *Idem.*

[45] *Ibid.*, p. 54.

[46] *Idem.*

[47] *Ibid.*, p. 49.

[48] Conrad Gesner, *Bibliotheca Universalis* . . . (Tiguri, 1545) and Raphael Volaterranus, *Opera*, new ed. (Lugduni, 1599). For Trithemius, see above, p. 5.

[49] Pits, *Relationum Historicarum*, p. 617.

[50] *Ibid.*, p. 589.

[51] *Ibid.*, p. 514.

⁵² Abraham Bzovius, *Historiae Ecclesiasticae,* 18 vols. (Cologne, 1616–27). Bzovius drew a part of his information from Nicholas Harpsfield, *Historiae Anglicana Ecclesiastica* . . . (Douais, 1622).

⁵³ Bzovius, *Historiae* (1618), XIV, col. 1202.

⁵⁴ In 1371 Wyclyf "erumpere in Anglia coepit, certa et immanis totius Catholicae religionis pestis." In 1377 Wyclyf "iam in apertum prodiens, venena in Ecclesiam spargegebat." *Ibid.,* cols. 1388 and 1556. [The quotations from this work have not been confirmed.]

⁵⁵ Bzovius, *Historiae* (1622), IV, 111.

⁵⁶ *Idem.*

⁵⁷ *Idem.*

⁵⁸ *Ibid.,* XV, 114.

⁵⁹ *Ibid.,* XV, 115. [Among the recent contributions to the analysis of Wyclyf as a philosopher should be noted: F. de Boor, *Wyclifs Simoniebegriff* (Halle: Niemeyer, 1970); H. Kaminsky, "Wyclifism as Ideology of Revolution," *Church History,* XXXII (1963), 57–74; G. Leff, *Heresy in the Later Middle Ages* (Manchester: Manchester University Press, 1967), II, 494–558; *idem,* "John Wyclif: The Path to Dissent," *Proceedings of the British Academy,* LII (1966), 143–80; *idem,* "Wyclif and the Augustinian Tradition, with Special Reference to His *De Trinitate,*" *Medievalia et Humanistica,* N.S., I (1970), 29–39; J. A. Robson, *Wyclif and the Oxford Schools* (Cambridge: Cambridge University Press, 1961); and M. J. Wilks, "The Early Oxford Wyclif: Papalist or Nominalist?," *Studies in Church History,* V (1969), 69–98.]

⁶⁰ "Alia praeterea multa quae probaverat in uno loco, in alio reprobat, memorando suis sectariis relicto exemplo, ut ipsi non tantum a seipsis, sed inter seipsos dissiderent." Bzovius, *Historiae* (1622), XV, 116.

⁶¹ Cum, inquit, (se. Guillelmus Witffordus) Oxonii, senteatias publice legeret Wiccleffus & postea cum esset Baccalauceus, ut appellant, responsalis, affirmabat accidentia quae vocant Sacramentalia, esse in subiecto: panis tamen substantiam nihilominus remanere. Sed cum urgentur: quidnam illa accidentia sustineret? post longam deliberationem, corpus mathematicum, respondit." *Ibid.,* XV, 115. A similar version was published by W. W. Shirley from MS. Bodl. 703, f. 129 r, containing Woodford's *Septuaginta duo questiones de sacramento Eucharistiae:* "Alias dum esset praedictus magister Johannes sententarius Oxoniae, ac etiam baccalarius responsalis, publice tenuit et in scholis quod licet accidentia sacramentalia, essent in subjecto, tamen quod panis in consecratione desinit esse. Et cum multae questiones essent sibi factae quid esset subjectum illorum accidentium, primo per tempus notabile respondit quod corpus mathematicum. Et posterius post multa argumenta sibi facta contra hoc respondit quod nescivit quid fuit subjectum illorum accedentium, bene tamen posuit quod habuerunt subjectum. Nunc in istis articulis et sua confessione ponit expresse quod panis manet post consecrationem, et est subjectum accidentium." *Fasciculi Zizaniorum Magistri Johannis Wyclif cum Tritico,* ed. W. W. Shirley (London: "Rolls Series", 1858), p. xv, note 4.

⁶² Bzovius, *Historiae* (1622), XV, 114.

⁶³ Wyclyf's *Trialogus* was published for the first time in Basel in 1525. [This publication "contained what is probably the first formal Reformation eulogy of Wycliffe . . . ." M. E. Aston, "John Wycliffe's Reformation Reputation," *Past and Present,* No. 30 (1965), 24. The political thought of Wyclyf has been the particular subject of such studies as M. E. Aston, "Lollardy and Sedition, 1381–1431," *Past and Present,* No. 17 (1960), pp. 1–44; L. J. Daly, *The Political Theory of John Wyclif* (Chicago: Loyola University Press, 1962); E. C. Tatnall, "John Wyclif and *Ecclesia Anglicana,*" *Journal of Ecclesiastical History,* XX (1969), 19–43; M. J. Wilks, "Predestination, Property and Power: Wyclif's Theory of Dominion and Grace," *Studies in Church History,* II (1965), 220–36; and *idem,* "*Reformatio Regni*: Wyclif and Hus as Leaders of Religious Protest Movements," *Ibid.,* IX (1972), 109–30. For Wyclif in government service, see J. H. Dahmus, "John Wyclif and the English Government," *Speculum,* XXXV (1960), 51–68; T. J. Hanrahan, "John Wyclif's Political Activity," *Mediaeval Studies,* XX

(1958), 154–66; and B. Smalley, "The Bible and Eternity: John Wyclif's Dilemma," *Journal of the Warburg and Courtauld Institutes,* XXVII (1964), 88–9.]

[64] Walsingham's *Ypodigma Neutriae* was published in London in 1574. His *Historia Anglicana* first appeared in London in 1594 and in Frankfurt in 1603. Roger Twysden edited *Knighton's Chronicle* in 1652, and Higden's *Polychronicon* was published in 1482, 1495 and 1527. The historians of this period are treated in Levi Fox, ed., *English Historical Scholarship in the Sixteenth and Seventeenth Centuries; . . .* (London: Published for the Dugdale Society by Oxford University Press, 1956).

[65] Otto Gierke, *Political Theories of the Middle Age,* tr. and intr. Frederic William Maitland (reprint; Boston: Beacon Press, 1958), p. viii.

[66] Francis Mason, *Vindiciae Ecclesiae Anglicanae . . . ,* 2nd ed. (London, 1625), p. 63.

[67] Samuel Clarke, *A Generall Martyrologie, . . .* (London, 1651). The introduction contains the following lines: "And amongst Histories, the Ecclesiasticall ought to have the preheminence, as being a glasse wherein all Christians may see by thousands of examples, both what they owe to God, and what they may expect from him" (sign. A 2 v.).

[68] *Ibid.,* p. 150.

[69] Luther is described as "undaunted," "the thunderbolt against the Pope." *Ibid.,* p. 156.

[70] *Ibid.,* sign. a 3 v., dedicatory poem "To the Reverend, the Author of the Book, Called *A Generall Martyrologie, &c.* By El. Cl."

[71] Samuel Taylor Coleridge eulogized Fuller in the following terms: "Wit was the stuff and substance of Fuller's intellect. It was the element, the earthen base, the material which he worked in, and this very circumstance has defrauded him of his due praise for the practical wisdom of the thoughts, for the beauty and variety of the truths, into which he shaped the stuff. Fuller was incomparably the most sensible, the least prejudiced, great man of an age that boasted a galaxy of great men." *Literary Remains* (London, 1836–9), II, 389–390.

[72] Thomas Fuller, *Abel Redevivus: Or, The Dead yet speaking, The Lives and Deaths of the Moderne Divines* (London, 1651).

[73] *Ibid.,* p. 9.

[74] *Idem.*

[75] *Ibid.,* p. 10.

[76] *Ibid.,* p. 11.

[77] Thomas Fuller, *The Church History of Britain: From the Birth of Jesus Christ untill the Year MDCXLVIII* (London, 1655). Fuller wrote about Wyclyf in *The Worthies of England,* ed. John Freeman (London: Allen and Unwin, 1952 [1662]), p. 155. There he said about him: "It is a great honour to this small county [Durham], that it produced the last maintainer of religion, before the general decay thereof; understand me, learned Bede; and the firm restorer thereof, I mean this Wycliffe, the subject of our present discourse."

[78] Fuller, *Church History,* Book IV, p. 129.

[79] *Ibid.,* p. 130.

[80] *Idem.*

[81] *Idem.*

[82] *Ibid.,* p. 131.

[83] *Ibid.,* pp. 131–4.

[84] *Ibid.,* p. 135.

[85] *Idem.*

[86] *Idem.*

[87] *Ibid.,* pp. 135–6.

[88] *Ibid.,* pp. 139, 141–2.

[89] *Ibid.,* p. 143.

[90] Roger Twysden, *An Historical Vindication of the Church of England in point of Schism . . . ,* ed. G. E. Corrie (Cambridge: University Press [1657], 1847), p. 96.

[91] *Ibid.*, pp. 234–240. [The quotation is found on p. 240.]

[92] Sir Robert Howard, *The History of the Reigns of Edward and Richard II; with reflections, and characters of their chief ministers and favourites* (London, 1690), p. 18.

[93] *Ibid.*, pp. 90, 94.

[94] Joshua Barnes, *The History of that Most Victorious Monarch Edward III^d King of England and France and Lord of Ireland, And First Founder of the Most Noble Order of the Garter* (Cambridge, 1688).

[95] The narrative contradicts the words of the dedication where Barnes speaks of "quiet and secure Government, Loyal Parliaments, . . . Eternal Felicities." *Ibid.*, sign. A 2 v.

[96] *Ibid.*, p. 902. There was new information in Anthony à Wood, *Historia et Antiquitates universitatis Oxoniensis,* 2 vols. (Oxford, 1674), I, 74–76, 193, and II, 72–73.

[97] Barnes, *Edward III*, p. 902.

[98] *Idem.*

[99] *Ibid.*, p. 903.

[100] *Ibid.*, p. 902.

[101] Gilbert Burnet, *The History of the Reformation of the Church of England,* 7 vols. (Oxford: Oxford University Press, 1829), I, Pt. ii, 45–6.

[102] *Ibid.*, I, Pt. ii, 46.

[103] *Ibid.*, I, Pt. ii, vii–viii.

[104] John Milton, *Of Reformation Touching Church-Discipline in England: And the Causes that hitherto have hindred it* (London, 1641), p. 13. Milton prefaces his conclusion in these words: "And it is still Episcopacie that before all our eyes worsens and sluggs the most learned, and seeming religious of our Ministers . . . ." *Idem.*

[105] Antoine Varillas, *Histoire du Wiclefianisme* (Lyon, 1682), sign. * 2 v. Varillas had "worthy" predecessors. The first in time was François de Belle-Forest, *Les Grandes Annales* . . . (Paris, 1579). This writer considered Wyclyf as "un fol-sage"; *ibid.*, p. 943. The account of Francis Godwin, bishop of Llandaff, *A Catalogue of the Bishops of England,* . . . (London, 1615) contains many unhistorical moments. See the execution of Archbishop Sudbury by the rebels in 1381; *ibid.*, p. 148. Varillas drew information from Louis Maimbourg, *Histoire du grand schisme d'Occident,* 2nd ed., 2 vols. (Paris, n.d.), I, 177–202 *passim.*

[106] Varillas, *Histoire du Wiclefianisme,* sign. * 2 v.

[107] *Ibid.*, p. 2.

[108] *Ibid.*, p. 8.

[109] *Ibid.*, pp. 14–15.

[110] *Ibid.*, pp. 15–28, *passim.*

[111] *Ibid.*, p. 39. Wyclyf "recuet [Ball] à bras ouverts, & luy permit apres deux ou trois conferences de prêcher sa doctrine."

[112] Antoine Varillas, *Histoire des Révolutions arrivées dans l'Europe en matière de Religion,* 4 vols. (Paris, 1686–88), I, sign. a ii r-v.

[113] *Ibid.*, I, 40.

[114] *Ibid.*, I, 47.

[115] *Ibid.*, I, 55.

[116] Gilbert Burnet, *Reflections on Mr. Varillas's History of the Revolutions that hapned [sic] in Europe in Matters of Religion. And more particularly on his Ninth Book that relates to England* (London, 1689), p. 3.

[117] *Ibid.*, p. 7.

[118] *Ibid.*, pp. 5, 61.

[119] *Ibid.*, p. 7.

[120] *Ibid.*, p. 8.

[121] *Ibid.*, p. 9.

[122] *Ibid.*, p. 32, citing Varillas, *Histoire des Révolutions,* II, 226.

[123] Burnet, *Reflections,* p. 63.

[124] Antoine Varillas, *Réponse de M. Varillas à la critique de M. Burnet sur les deux premiers tomes de l'Histoire des révolutions arrivées dans l'Europe en matière de Religion* (Paris, 1687), sign. * 2 v: "Mais, Sire, il s'en prend à *Vôtre Majesté*; et par une

audace incomprehensible il l'attaqua d'une maniére si outrageuse, que la Postérité ne pourra jamais s'étonner assez que l'on ait permis les impressions & le débit d'un si méchant Livre.

"Mais la maniére la plus héroïque de repousser la calomnie quand elle s'attache aux Personnes les plus élevées dans le monde, n'est pas de lui repartir, ni de la representer telle qu'elle est. C'est, Sire, de la mépriser, ..."

[125] *Ibid.*, pp. 2–5.

[126] Gilbert Burnet, *A Defence of the Reflections on the ninth book of the first volum* [*sic*] *Of Mr. Varillas's History of Heresies. Being a reply to his Answer* (Amsterdam, 1687), pp. 89–92.

[127] It should be understood that not Wyclyf but the Reformation as a whole was the central point of the debate.

[128] Daniel de Larroque, *Nouvelles accusations contre M. Varillas, ou Remarques critiques contre une partie de son premier livre de l'Histoire de l'hérésie* (Amsterdam, 1687), pp. 12–13.

[129] *Ibid.*, p. 14.

[130] *Ibid.*, pp. 15–16.

[131] *Ibid.*, pp. 18–25.

[132] *Ibid.*, p. 27.

[133] *Ibid.*, pp. 35–42.

[134] *Ibid.*, p. 47.

[135] *Ibid.*, p. 60.

[136] *Ibid.*, p. 70.

[137] *Ibid.*, p. 94.

[138] *Ibid.*, p. 95.

[139] *Idem.*

[140] *Ibid.*, p. 97.

[141] *Ibid.*, p. 98.

[142] *Ibid.*, p. 99.

[143] *Idem.*

[144] William King, *Reflections upon Mr. Varillas his History of Heresy* . . . (n.p., 1688), sign. A 2 v.

[145] *Ibid.*, sign. A 2.

[146] *Ibid.*, p. 41.

[147] *Idem.*

[148] Jacques-Bénigne Bossuet, *Histoire des variations des Églises protestantes*, 6th ed., 2 vols. (Paris, 1718), II, 60.

[149] *Ibid.*, II, 156.

[150] *Ibid.*, II, 159.

[151] *Idem.*

[152] *Idem.*

[153] *Ibid.*, II, 160.

[154] *Idem.*

[155] *Ibid.*, II, 162.

[156] Gilbert Burnet, *A Letter to Mr. Thevenot. Containing a censure of Mr. Le Grand History of King Henry the Eighth's Divorce. To which is added, a Censure of Mr. De Meaux's History of the Variations of the Protestant Churches. Together with Some further reflections on Mr. Le Grand* (London, 1689), p. 23.

[157] *Ibid.*, p. 20.

[158] Henrich Ludolff Benthem, *Engländischer Kirch- und Schulen-Staat* (Lüneburg, 1694), pp. 10, 54, 65, 543–4.

[159] *Ibid.*, p. 306.

[160] *Idem.*

[161] Richard Baxter, *Church-History of the Government of Bishops and their Councils Abbreviated* (London, 1680), cited words are on the title page.

[162] *Ibid.*, p. 431.

[163] *Ibid.*, p. 432.

[164] *Ibid.*, p. 433.

[165] Jan Amos Komenský, *Haggaeus redivivus* (Prague: Kalich, 1952), p. 23.

[166] Jan Amos Komenský, *Ksaft umirajici Matky Jednoty Bratrske,* ed. Fr. Bily ("Pestra knihovna"; Prague: Hynek, 1912), p. 109.

[167] Bohuslav Balbin, *Epitome historica rerum bohemicarum* . . . (Prague, 1677), p. 402.

[168] Bohuslav Balbin, *Dissertatio apologetica pro lingua slavonica praecipue bohemica,* ed. and tr. Emanuel Tonner (Prague, 1869). Balbin's watchword was "In silentio et spe fortitudo mea." *Ibid.,* p. lii.

[169] The psalmodic tenor of Balbin's *Dissertatio apologetica* betrays the anguish of the author.

[170] Komensky, *Ksaft,* p. 89.

[171] John Milton, *Of Reformation Touching Church-Discipline in England: And the Causes that hitherto have hindred it* (London, 1641), p. 13.

[172] *Ibid.,* p. 16.

[173] *Ibid.,* p. 62.

[174] *Ibid.,* p. 8.

[175] John Milton, *Animadversions upon the Remonstrants Defence, Against Smectymnuus* (London, 1641), p. 36.

[176] John Milton, *Areopagitica: a speech of Mr. John Milton For the Liberty of Unlicens'd Printing, To the Parliament of England* (London, 1644), p. 31.

[177] Lord Macaulay, *Works,* 12 vols. (London: Longmans, 1898), VIII, 202: "In the fourteenth century, the first and perhaps the greatest of the reformers, John Wickliffe, had stirred the public mind to its inmost depths."

Chapter

3

The Break With the Past

In the eighteenth century the Western world abandoned the ideals which had formed its *Weltanschauung* for centuries and decided to measure the destinies of men and states according to new standards. The idea of progress with its corresponding belief in the infinite perfectibility of man took hold of the best minds and intoxicated them with visions which far surpassed anything Potemkin was able to present to his empress. Religion did not disappear; only its dominant rule over society came to an end. Revelation had, since the appearance of the "incomparable Mr. Locke," lost its virtue among the enthroned and reigning senses, and among those who molded the thoughts of that age did not count any more. The Catholic Church, believed to be the repository of superstition and opponent of progress, was identified as *infâme* by a man who himself became a living god, and launched the appeal to destroy it. Eighteenth-century intellectuals broke away, unconcerned by traditions, from the past and began to reassess those values which were cherished by the former society. In this new period Wyclyf was looked at, especially on the Continent, with new eyes. The old unfavorable judgments were interpreted under the changed circumstances as words of praise.

The eighteenth century was the century of dictionaries, encyclopaedias, catalogues, and works of synthesis. These had their remote predecessors in the many *Mirrors of the Heretics* and the catalogues of ecclesiastical writers already mentioned. Their immediate forerunner was the *Dictionary* of Moréri which, if we consider the number of editions it went through in eighty-five years, testifies to the new spirit of inquiry.[1] It cannot surprise us therefore to find in the seventeen hundreds the name of Wyclyf in the new media. It may be more surprising to discover that in the eighteenth century his name was no longer excluded as it had been when he was considered a heretic, from the class of "ecclesiastical writers." In 1693 Msgr. Louis Ellies-Dupin thus summarized the new temper: "Un Auteur qui combat une Heresie de son temps, & qui a des contestations personnelles avec ceux qu'il attaque, s'exprime bien autrement que celui qui écrit contre une Heresie éteinte, qui ne prend aucune part à cette querelle, & qui n'a point en écrivant d'autre motif, que de defendre la verité."[2] This view, which Ellies-Dupin affirms in his *Nouvelle bibliothèque des auteurs ecclésiastiques,* led him to portray Wyclyf without passion, dramatic exclamations, or gross perversion of truth. On the other hand, Ellies-Dupin, who professed the belief that criticism is the flame which enlightens us and leads us in the dark paths of antiquity, was not an entirely original observer.[3] Noting that Wyclyf had been ejected from Canterbury Hall, he subscribed to the old view: "Ainsi Wiclef fut obligé de ceder: cette disgrace l'indisposa contre la Cour de Rome, & lui fit chercher les moïens de s'en venger."[4] Ellies-Dupin accepted the text of Gregory XI's bulls at face value, and linked Wyclyf to Marsilius of Padua and Jean Jandun, "& de quelques autres Auteurs qui avoient écrit de la Puissance Ecclesiastique, & temporelle suivant les interêts des Princes, contre les prétentions des Papes . . . ."[5] He makes Wyclyf blindly follow all the excesses into which these authors had fallen ("il encherit encore par dessus") and preach publicly against the jurisdiction of the pope and the bishops.[6]

Ellies-Dupin's chronology was impeccable; he distinguished the two trials at St. Paul's and Lambeth and assigned them to their proper time and space. He gave 31 December 1384 as the day on which Wyclyf died, thus setting aside the Catholic Walsingham, and accepted the dating of the Protestants Stow and Wood.[7] Ellies-Dupin exculpated Wyclyf from any participation in the Peasants's Revolt, though the possibility that his teaching might have been a contributory factor did not escape him. Like Bossuet he read the *Trialogus,* but dismissed the work with the dry comment that "Le stile de cet Ouvrage est sec & scholastique, il y a peu de justesse & beaucoup de prévention & d'emportement dans ses raisonnements."[8] In critical acumen he was one step ahead of Larroque, who was convinced that Wyclyf was the author of the *Wyclif's Wicket,* or *La petite Port de Wiclef.* Ellies-Dupin destroyed the legend by pointing out that the tract was written in 1395, and came from the pen of one of Wyclyf's disciples.[9] He read Ortuinus Gratius, and knew that in 1396 Widford [*sic*] defended the condemnations of the Council of London, not by scholastic reasonings but by authorities taken from the Holy Scriptures, the Fathers and canon law. Ellies-Dupin judges this treatise as "solide & sçavant pour ce temps-là, quoi qu'il [treatise] ne soit pas bien écrit."[10] Ellies-Dupin is a refreshing writer, a man on the crossroads of history, imbued with traditions of the past yet receptive to new thoughts. His vision and understanding are more comprehensive than the enlightened iconoclasts, who would have never stepped down from the pedestal of the *siècle des lumières* to agree with Ellies-Dupin: "Le Quatorzième Siècle fournit une diversité de matières assez agréable."[11]

In the same category it is convenient to place Claude Fleury, another French writer with ecclesiastical background and sympathies. As in the case of Ellies-Dupin, Fleury did not hate in order to write. His *Histoire ecclésiastique,* published for the first time between 1690 and 1719, is devoid of name-calling.[12] What he did is more impressive and more durable. With a dry sense of humor *à l'anglaise* he sought out arguments to repudiate or weaken with what seems to be a brush of his hand. Fleury is always conscious of the importance of literary effect, and he never tires of emphasizing it explicitly or by innuendo. When he approaches the five bulls of condemnation and the nineteen articles, he takes number XII under sharp Gallican eyes and pronounces *sine ira et studio*: "Je ne vois point que ce dernier article soit condamnable."[13] He is aware of Wyclyf's *Protestatio* (delivered to justify views on the Church), but managed to stay outside the issue, which undoubtedly seemed to him far-fetched and foreign, with an explanatory sentence which matched the obscure medieval virtuosity of Wyclyf himself.[14] On the other hand, Fleury was not as keen an historian as Ellies-Dupin; he did not handle his sources with the same care. Wyclyf's death again is mistakenly set on 31 December 1387— after an agony of two years starting on 29 December 1385[15]—and Fleury followed previous historians by turning John Ball into a disciple of Wyclyf.[16] As to the peasant rebellion, Fleury excluded Wyclyf completely, made John Ball an accessory before the act, and drew into the picture both the *seigneurs* and the people they abused.[17] Fleury points out, as a matter of fact, that the maxims of this ignorant priest were aimed at upsetting civil society.[18] And then, to show that his knowledge of the Scriptures was superior to that of "ce prêtre ignorant," he said that it was wrong to believe that servitude was contrary to the will of God, and quoted with relish seven passages from Exodus 22.2–3, and the Epistle of St. Peter II.18 to support his statement. He, too, read the *Trialogus*. His impression did not diverge considerably from his two contemporaries: "C'est comme un corps de théologie, qui contient tout le venim de sa doctrine."[19] Fleury was an aristocrat of the robe, not an apologist. He wrote from pleasure, anger and high blood pressure being conspicuously absent.

When one surveys historical literature of the end of the seventeenth century one is amazed to discover the number of allusions to a theoretical basis of history. After the wars of the first half of the seventeenth century, which started as religious crusades and finished as a political bargain, the trend in the latter part is towards the abstract. Truth suddenly appears as the supreme moral criterion. This notion creeps surreptitiously into historical works at first, concealed in sentences which are nothing but *obiter dicta*. But, step by step, the tendency to be impartial, to present truth (to be understood as the last refuge of the intellectuals after the exodus of religion) is advertised more boldly, and assumes the proportions of a manifesto. But, under the first impact of the new, creative formula, it was not yet realized that truth could be incomplete.

This devotion to an assumed perfect truth is more amply displayed in the works of German writers than in those of French or English origin. Gottfried Arnold prefaced the *Unpartheyische Kirchen- und Ketzer-Historie* with a conception of history which encompasses almost all the postulates of nineteenth-century historiography, and which has the advantage of a more entertaining vein.[20] Those were the times when an author could convince unbelievers with arguments such as these: "Was in denen zwey letzten *seculis* vor *manuscripta* angefuhret worden, bin ich erbotig einem jeden, der es nothig hat und verlanget, dieselben *privatim* zu zeigen und als *genuina* zu *legitimiren.*"[21] Unfortunately there were no manuscripts available to Arnold on the fourteenth century and the life of John Wyclyf. But it is not the facts that really matter in 1699, and in the three following editions in the eighteenth century. It is more the spirit, the temper and the mood which attract a twentieth-century historian. Arnold found qualities in Wyclyf which he openly admired: Wyclyf fought the shameful tyranny of the pope and his clergy because they assumed divine authority and held God and His will for nothing.[22] For Arnold this was the important aspect of Wyclyf's life. He knew that Wyclyf held "viele unreine meynungen" but he rejected the legitimacy of any censure by the explanation that under the circumstances which then existed it certainly was no wonder.[23] Arnold knew Wyclyf's enemies ascribed to him *offt wunderliche lehrsatze* but was it not, he asked, the habit of all *Katzermacher*?[24] In fact, he continues, are not these allegations denied by the beneficial effect Wyclyf's work so often had, and thus proof he was looking towards God and His honor? The forty-five condemned articles, he says, redound really to Wyclyf's glory since they witness how deep an insight God had given him "in die greuel der Clerisey."[25] In addition, they were eminently successful: they led to the outbreak of the Hussite wars. In Arnold's extraordinary interpretation of Wyclyf (especially the condemned articles at Constance) we detect signs of many European currents. Is not Arnold a German Voltaire, albeit standing on a different level, and is he not united with the Frenchman in the opposition to religious tyranny, in the belief in the existence of God and the condemnation of complicated religious dogmas?

There were, however, other ideologies in the galaxy of eighteenth-century ideas. Pierre Bayle stands alone with his *Dictionnaire historique et critique*: he had no direct followers.[26] It is a pity that Bayle did not include Wyclyf in his *Dictionary*. Exercising his historical abilities in the text, and opening his mind in the footnotes, he might have thrown unusual light on the reformer; but Wyclyf appears only casually. In the article on William Wickham, which is neither brilliant nor dull, he mentioned the secondhand information that Wickham took part in the condemnation of Wyclyf at Oxford.[27] This gave Bayle the opportunity to air his opinion on the bishop's intelligence. From the phrasing of the short paragraph, however, one does not get a clear impression as to what Bayle really thought: did he praise or did he condemn Wickham for the part played in Oxford? Bayle had his *lacunae,* too. He did not question the accuracy of Varillas's statement that Wyclyf coveted the bishopric of Winchester; he only concluded that Wickham was never deprived of his see between 1367 and 1404. Thus convinced, he dismissed Varillas's account of the origin of Wyclyf's heresy without adding anything to our knowledge himself.

Antoine Varillas's *Wiclefianisme* is one of the most extraordinary specimens to prove the adage that books have their own lives and peculiar destinies. After an ignominious burial in the sixteen-eighties, when it collapsed under the joint attacks of Larroque and Burnet, it rose (in disguise) from the dead in England, revived in English translation by an Anglican presbyter, designed to combat the views of the Lutherans, Calvinists, and "Wickliffians." Matthias Earbery complained that they all "are our secret Enemies, while they pretend to be on our Side: They envy the beauty of our *Sion,* and would see her Glories buried in the Dust."[28] Earbery remarks that epithets such as "Scarlet Whore" and "Antichristian Beasts" were not unusual to designate the Anglican Church and its members.[29] Wyclyf was singled out from the start as a wicked man, and Earbery claimed to have the evidence to support the charge. Wyclyf's cause, the author says, "was first patroniz'd by one who endeavoured to be a vile Usurper, and by an Whore; and was carried on by no better Means to its Period."[30] Earbery repeated the old accusation, of which Wyclyf's critics never grow tired, namely that he started his seditious movement as a matter of revenge for the loss of a bishopric, and promised to the reader that with his book a scene will be opened to a "View entirely new."[31] We have become acquainted with the scene already, and its contours are familiar. But there remains the question why despite Earbery's explanatory remarks he solicits interest in such a concentrated, massive and hostile offensive against the Wyclyfites, who did not even form a recognized sect. Why are the "Bigoted Papists" and "Latitudinarian Protestants" lumped together and condemned in terms which sound like ramblings of an unbalanced religious conservative?[32] The reason is supplied on the first text page of the preface: there are too many Protestants and the term got confused.[33] Earbery's attack implied that some Protestants were more respectable than others, and, as was customary, Wyclyf provided the impetus to follow the attack through to its logical conclusion. Earbery's passionate words reveal to us that the English Protestants were then sharply divided, and among them especially the Anglicans were uncertain of their position.

The attempt to redress the balance in favor of Wyclyf was undertaken by John Lewis, and his rehabilitation of the same John Wyclyf, who was in the eighteenth century the victim of the most vicious denigration of his historical stature, starts a new era in the study of Wyclyf.[34] It is true that a large portion of the material Lewis used was rediscovered in the seventeenth century by the Oxford men who infused new blood into the old and seemingly lifeless body; it is true that many primary sources, especially the accounts of Walsingham, Knighton, and Malverne, the continuator of *Polychronicon,* were available; but until John Lewis they were not used properly. It is equally true that the study of diplomatics was a recent discipline, and the archives were not the most pleasant places to spend a day, but it is the merit of Lewis that he overcame difficulties to represent Wyclyf as he really was and we must believe Lewis that it cost him pains and expense, as he remarks.[35]

A superficial look at the sources which Lewis used—he calls them testimonies—is a revealing experience. Some of his authors are not regarded today as worth mentioning, and probably for the demands of "scientific" and "objective" history they are not: as, for example, John Jewell, bishop of Salisbury (1560–71); but nobody may dispute the depth of Lewis's preparation for his task of setting aright the reputation of Wyclyf so much damaged by a "pretended *Presbyter of the Church of England,*" and "such a confused Mass of Ignorance and Scurrility."[36]

It would be long indeed to pass in review all the accomplishments of Lewis, and the freshness of his work. The list of the facts which appeared for the first time is lengthy. He first described Wyclyf's early years in Oxford, and assigned dates to his university career. He was the first to inform us that his benefices included Fillingham, Ludger-shall, and Aust. Lewis brought out the information that Wyclyf took part in the negotiations at Bruges in 1374, and this provided the reason for the close connection with the royal house that tied him in political matters to the royal policy. He deciphered the complicated zig-zag script of events after 1381, and he reintroduced into the narrative, for the first time since the days of Foxe, the vicissitudes of Wyclyf's followers in Oxford.[37] This handful of Lewis's contributions for the better understanding of Wyclyf, which could be greatly increased, is composed only of the correct results of his research.

Even Lewis was neither infallible, nor omniscient. Relying on the Parker manuscripts in Corpus Christi College, Cambridge, which in-cluded English tracts against the friars believed to originate from Wyc-lyf's pen, he followed earlier Protestant hagiography and made Wyclyf the terror of the mendicants.[38] Lewis's faith in this tradition was so strong he cast aspersions on the reported presence of the friars at the trial.[39] On the prosecutions, trials or just hearings of 1377 and 1378 we find Lewis patently wrong, seldom as it may happen. However, the explanation for the statement that Wyclyf faced his interrogators twice at the order of the pope may lie in Lewis's sincere belief that the English clergy were incapable of initiating proceedings against another English priest.[40]

Lewis was the first man who endeavored to establish Wyclyf's date of birth, but it will remain a mystery forever. Without explanation, he decided upon 1324, and that date became an immediate success and an heirloom of historical research to be passed down from generation to generation. All the followers of Lewis in this respect remained obliv-ious of the fact that the date was surrounded by two qualifications. Lewis said quite modestly that ''John Wicliffe was born, very proba-bly, about the Year MCCCXXIV.''[41]

The second edition of Lewis's work appeared in 1723. What is in-teresting in the new edition, is the Advertisement—a ten-page argu-ment against the opponents of Wyclyf (''a Rebel, and an impious Man''), who were led by the antiquary Thomas Hearne, the man who did so much to preserve knowledge of the past, even unpleasant past, to the public in England.[42] In the eighteenth century, however, diver-sity of opinions was such that the words ''rebel and impious man'' lose their pristine significance, and we are at a loss to know what irritated Thomas Hearne so much and so constantly.

England had in the eighteenth century at least two scholarly works which provided information without premeditated bias. William Cave's *Scriptorum ecclesiasticorum historia literaria,* to which Henry Wharton wrote an appendix covering what is called today the later Middle Ages, was standard reference work for that class of people for whom religion was a part of the intellectual's occupation. This is the impression one gets from the polished version of Wyclyf's life and works by Henry Wharton. There are very few facts, included only to frame an interpretation to Wyclyf wherein opinions and personal sallies, worded in a precious style, are frequent. This rococo style is masterly in the article on Wyclyf: it is a series of compliments, some of them grossly exaggerated. Wharton went beyond the praise of Knighton: "Vir erat, quo majorem non tulit postremis hisce saeculis Christianus orbis; quique non minus supra laudem quam invidiam positus videtur."[43] Despite Wharton's respect for the documents of the Middle Ages (which produced the *Anglia Sacra,* a compilation which has not yet fully been superseded) he did not eliminate feelings, but produced an eulogy of Wyclyf's knowledge of municipal laws—of which we know nothing. Another reason for praising Wyclyf was the discovery that in Wyclyf's works there is nothing puerile, nothing dull: everything is grave and serene. Wharton's historical capability is demonstrated in his remarks on the documents which he read. Here his penetrating mind reduced the old argument to new and more correct proportions. It was Wharton who was convinced that Wyclyf's so-called recantation meant hardly less than a continuation of his old stand with different means. He also relegated the *Ostiolum Wiclefi* to its correct authorship: "Hallucinatus autem est, quisquis libelli titulo apposuit, cum anno 1395 scriptum esse. Ante septennium enim obierat Wiclefus."[44] He stabbed Varillas, who was on nearly everybody's lips when the *Scriptorum ecclesiasticorum historia literaria* was published, and assigned him the titles *historicus mendacissimus* and *putidissimus impostor.*[45] He listed Wyclyf's works, but only copies he read or saw, the Bible among them. Copies of the latter he located at Emmanuel College, Cambridge, the Cotton Library, and Royal Library.[46] Despite the gentle words he used Wharton did not think very much about Wyclyf and did not understand him. The result is a portrait which, though composed of many acute observations, is too flat, and its praise too mechanical to make it impressive.

Thomas Tanner's *Bibliotheca Britannico-Hibernica* (1748), as the title page says, *opus utilissimum, et XL annorum studio ac industria elaboratum,* is more useful for its detailed footnotes than the text which Tanner, a great admirer, together with David Wilkins, of John Leland the antiquarian, borrowed from the latter's *Commentaries.* It is difficult not to advance the opinion that Leland's account of Wyclyf, which combines healthy respect for his knowledge with doubts concerning the sense of his attacks on the dogmatic bulwarks of the Church, expressed the feelings of the bishop of St. Asaph himself. It was still fashionable to regard Wyclyf's attacks on the friars as praiseworthy, but as to the rest there was only one judgment: "O factum bene! si intra hos prudens se continuisset limites."[47] The footnotes which complete the text are of mixed origin. Bale, of course, supplied the greatest number of *incipits*, but Wharton was not neglected, and Tanner himself cited locations and names of manuscripts. Tanner had in mind a collection of latest information concerning the writers of the British Isles. That he took Leland for his guide is an indication of the growing interest in and respect for the past. Tanner steered the middle, writing for all and offending no one. As it so often happens in works of this nature, there is a singular omission in the authorities. Neither John Lewis's work nor his printed documents are mentioned at all.

It would not be correct to assume that the new trend of writing about ecclesiastical matters in general and Wyclyf in particular, with the personality of the writer either concealed behind the veil of manuscript sources or shifting the stress from religion to erudition, was the only way to express one's views on a subject which by its nature called for a variety of the most diverging opinions. The dictionaries very often embody narratives which unmistakably betray religious sympathies of a certain kind. And this was done when the dictionaries were destined for general circulation, and the publishers were aware that they came into the hands of an assortment of many different and peculiar citizens. In the *Biographica Britannica*, published between 1747–1766, the history of John Wyclyf is given a lavish background (with the rays of Lewis reflected from the pages), and a distinctive atmosphere. The facts need not detain us. They were scarcely more exact than those found anywhere else. The date 1324, the prebend at Aust, all the recent research of the century are wedged at appropriate places in the condensed narrative. It is increased moreover by the inclusion of the so-called friar episode which, just like Fuller's Avon and Swift peroration, found its way without difficulty into the nineteenth-century biographies of Wyclyf.[48] In the eighteenth century the ancient friars still caused high temperatures. "Bigots" attacked Wyclyf in the summer of 1381 when he began attacking transubstantiation, "the very gainful and favorite, though the most absurd and impudent doctrine."[49] And an appended note explains what the doctrine of transubstantiation was: "It tended to exalt the mystical and wonder-working power of the Popish priest, and to make them thought something more than men, when they could make God," and "for the hard names given him by T. Walden, T. Walsingham, N. Harpsfield, &c. they are the revilings of bigots, and prejudiced enemies. The devoted slaves to the court of Rome that could burn his bones, will not spare his memory.''[50]

We do not know the author of the article but whoever he was, the engrained hostility towards Rome, manifested by the choice of the words, such as bigot, proved that the Enlightenment could make common cause in many respects with the Protestant inheritance, and satisfy both its irreligious adherents and the keepers of the religious tradition.

But this new age (God its perfect watchmaker) and ideology centered around magnetic fields of reason and natural rights, did not leave any positive impression on the Church. The faithful may have borrowed words from the *philosophes,* and they may have listened with more than studied interest to connected social doctrines—especially at the lower levels of the hierarchy—but official teaching was not modified in the least. However, the tenor of Catholic writing proves that their press was unaffected by alarms from the world outside.

Moréri's *Le Grand Dictionnaire,* in print from 1674 to at least 1759, presents the standard Catholic view: Wyclyf was a heresiarch, and there were no mitigating circumstances to review the judgment.[51] Even though correct presentation of facts testifies to the reputation of Lewis's book in France, the interpretation remained untouched. St. Augustine is defended against the allegation that Wyclyf followed him to such a degree that his disciples styled him ''Jean-Augustin Wiclef''; but besides this fascinating bit the editor of the 1759 edition, M. Drouet, repeated the old indictments: Wyclyf incited the peasants to commit innumerable disturbances ''en criant à pleine tête, *Liberté,*'' and for this Drouet hurls at them the unflattering epithets ''ces rustres'' and ''cette canaille.'' This relatively short notice ends with the wrong date of Wyclyf's death, but this is an insignificant shortcoming in an article which aims more at accusing than understanding.[52]

Another specimen of Catholic critique is the *Grosses vollständiges Universal Lexicon aller Wissenschaften* published in 1748 by the Royal Prussian *Commercial Rath* Johann Heinrich Zedler.[53] Dedicating the work in characteristic effusive terms to the ''Most Worthy Prince and Lord Angelus Maria Quirino,'' a cardinal and prefect of the *Congregatio dell'Indice,* Zedler signed himself in very small letters as ''unterthänigster Knecht.''[54] The treatment reserved to Wyclyf is fair; no effort is made to unleash a vituperative offensive.[55] Zedler not only mastered all the known sources of his times (reliance on Cave is clear throughout) but he also cited works which have disappeared completely even from the bibliographies of the most antiquarian books.[56] His crowning achievement was the discussion of the forty-five articles condemned at Constance. Zedler divided them into two categories: good and bad. Among the good ones (and one cannot suppress amazement considering that the encyclopaedia is dedicated to a cardinal) is first of all the denial of transubstantiation.[57] He also argues that the right of deposing the pope is equally a good article.[58] Only then does he enumerate the "böse Artikel," beginning with Wyclyf's denial of the real presence in the sacrament of the altar. Such confrontation—this "bad" article against the first "good" one—strikes one immediately, and reconciliation is not helped by Zedler's reticence.[59]

Do we have here a Protestant who is Catholic, or a Catholic who has Protestant sympathies? Or are we face to face with an extremely skillful dissembler who puts forward like Abelard the *Sic* and *Non*, leaving a choice to the taste of the reader? The mystery is compounded by the enigmatic silence of Cardinal Quirino, prefect of the *Congregatio dell'Indice*. A permissible speculation may be that the cardinal had not read volume forty-six, and that Zedler took liberties with the subject, contrary to his apparent respect for the cardinal. In the eighteenth century everything may have been possible, and a double allegiance was not an impossibility, although one would like to know the reasons that led Zedler to adopt two different sets of religious values in a work published under Catholic patronage. Zedler's help to the study of Wyclyf was of the kind which disturbs the mind.

Whatever one may think of the great protagonists of the Enlightenment, as for example Voltaire in France and Hume in England, one cannot deny that they were free from intellectual duplicity, and devoted to the ideals of which they were the torchbearers. The *Essai sur les moeurs*, typical of Voltaire's work, is a general history of the world seen through the eyes of a man whose opinion of history is well summarized in his own words: "Un esprit juste, en lisant l'histoire, n'est presque occupé qu'à la réfuter."[60] In brief, to refute for Voltaire means really to rewrite. Nor did he hesitate to rewrite the history of Wyclyf. For Voltaire the early Middle Ages were an age of darkness (*ignorance*) since they were under the yoke of the Church.[61] But the universities engendered doctors, and these persons, possessed of "l'envie de se signaler," began to examine mysteries which "pour le bien de la paix, devaient être toujours derrière un voile."[62] And the doctor who tore the veil most energetically was John Wyclyf, a doctor (the word has special significance in the vocabulary of Voltaire inasmuch as education was one of the keys to Progress) of the University of Oxford.[63]

Voltaire lists some of the views advocated by Wyclyf, showing what Voltaire considered most praiseworthy: the suppression of the papacy;

the impossibility of having accidents without subjects; the abolition of confession, indulgences and ecclesiastical hierarchy. Clearly Voltaire thought that everything that the Valdensians taught in secret, Wyclyf taught in public; that, with a few exceptions his doctrine was that of the Protestants and—strangely enough—of more than one society established far back in the past. Wyclyf's work was not done in vain: "Ces ouvrages pénétrèrent en Bohême, pays naguère barbare, qui de l'ignorance la plus grossière commençait à passer à cette autre espèce d'ignorance qu'on appelait alors *érudition*."[64] After this introduction Voltaire passed to John Hus, and commented on the barbarian nature of the fifteenth century.[65]

In England, recollecting the motives which led him to historical work, David Hume wrote slightly more than two months before his death: "I thought that I was the only historian that had at once neglected present power, interest, and authority, and the cry of popular prejudices; and as the subject [Hume's *History of England*] was suited to every capacity, I expected proportional applause."[66] The applause did not come at once, nor was Hume so disinterested to be unaffected by "present power, interest, and authority." His lines dealing with John Wyclyf provide another proof for philosophers of history who claim that objective history is beyond the pale of the historian's capability, however many verbal assurances he may give. This charge is well illustrated in the case of Hume, of whom Adam Smith said: "His temper, indeed, seemed to be more happily balanced, if I may be allowed such an expression, than that perhaps of any other man I have ever known."[67]

Hume wrote about Wyclyf as befitted the typical representative of the age of reason and rational explanation. Using the common language of the enlightened intelligentsia, he could not shed the atmosphere he helped to shape: "The disgust, which the laity had received from the numerous usurpations both of the court of Rome, and of their own clergy, had weaned the kingdom very much from *superstition* [italics added]."[68] The word "heretic" never appears. Wyclyf "seems to have been a man of parts and learning; and has the honour of being the first person in Europe, who publickly called in question those doctrines, which had universally passed for certain and undisputed during so many ages."[69] Learning and scepticism are the two qualities Hume admired most in Wyclyf.[70] He considered his "remarkable austerity of life and manners," an aspect of Wyclyf's life which Walsingham and his *sequaces* condemned as an aspect of hypocrisy, and came to a despiritualized explanation of it which does not allow that religion might have been at least partially responsible for Wyclyf's behavior and stand. For Hume it was:

> a circumstance common to almost all those who dogmatize in any new way, both because men, who draw to them the attention of the public, and expose themselves to the odium of great multitudes, are obliged to be very guarded in their conduct, and because few, who have a strong propensity to pleasure or business, will enter upon so difficult and laborious an undertaking. [71]

Hume was convinced, as Voltaire was, that Wyclyf's doctrines were essentially those of the sixteenth-century reformers: "He only carried some of them farther than was done by the more sober part of these reformers." [72]

It is instructive to compare the selection from Wyclyf's tenets made by Hume with that made by Voltaire. Hume indicated to his readers first of all that Wyclyf had denied the real presence, supremacy of the Church of Rome, and the merit of monastic vows. He then listed Wyclyf's beliefs in the Scriptures, the dependence of the church on the state and the poverty of the clergy. Evidently he endorsed the view that the begging friars "were a general nuisance" and should not have been supported. Hume did not leave out the disputable notion, ascribed to Wyclyf, that everything was subject to fate and destiny, and insisted that in Wyclyf's opinion all men were predestined. [73] It may be seen how the traditional English Protestant view concerning the monks and friars was sacrosanct for Hume, and how Wyclyf's fatalism—close enough to Hume's conception of the universe—was pleasant to his ear. The English philosopher also had no trouble elucidating some of the difficulties appearing in the texts and articles. The "tortured meanings" are there "to render them quite innocent and inoffensive." [74] Characterizing Wyclyf in a final paragraph, he exhibits clearly his eighteenth-century rationalistic English origin: "From the whole of his doctrines, Wickliffe appears to have been strongly tinctured with enthusiasm, and to have been thereby the better qualified to oppose a church, whose distinguishing character was superstition." [75]

Hume touched on the problem of why Wyclyf's views were not accepted and put into effect; alluding to the continuity of progress in history, Hume expressed the confidence that he lived in the best possible times. His last words on Wyclyf are unequivocal: "But tho' the age seemed strongly disposed to receive them [Wyclyf's views], affairs were not yet fully ripe for this great revolution; and the finishing blow to ecclesiastical power was reserved to a period of more curiosity, literature, and inclination for novelties." [76] Hume was more subtle than

Voltaire. Both of them, however, were convinced that the Church was dead.

It would be a serious mistake were Condorcet to be omitted from the short list of the great lights of the Enlightenment. In many ways he speaks for the whole movement; he expresses the aspirations of the *philosophes* and their unbounded faith in progress. In the *Esquisse,* written in jail in expectation of death at the hands of those for whom he was preparing a better world, he did not despair or abandon his beliefs. Consolidating them in an historical program, outlining the successive stages through which mankind has to pass before it will reach the earthly paradise in which understanding, harmony and a good life without precedent would be its only fruits, he described the pains of each of the ten stages into which he divided history, and underlined the importance of sporadically there appearing individuals (or whole movements) who struggled for a better world while suffering the evil of the old. Here Wyclyf is remembered, not as the flower of fourteenth-century Oxford philosophy, but as the spiritual leader of the Peasants's Rebellion in 1381.[77] Condorcet certainly defends Wyclyf in the latter's position on disendowment of the Church.[78] Everything was justified that was done for progress. With this view, Condorcet, devoid of Christianity, nevertheless pardoned his own death to the executioners, and made a revolution the voice of God heard through means other than religion.

It was stated at the beginning of this chapter that the eighteenth century burned many bridges connecting it with the past and started to build a new universe on new grounds and new territory. At the same time evidence was adduced to show that the old institutions resisted the process of decay which was being forced on them and defended their right to live and their many traditions; the traditional view that Wyclyf was a heretic was held with tenacity. We have also drawn attention to the fact that the variety of opinions sprouting with unrestrained vigor all over Europe brought to light the confusion and dilemmas of religious history, especially affecting those neither quite sophisticated enough nor quite sufficiently religious. With a few illustrations of these several trends this chapter on the eighteenth century will be carried to its end.

Catholic literature of this century surely displays the great decline of intellectual power in the Church since the halcyon days of the sixteenth and seventeenth centuries, for the great irony of the eighteenth century is that, while the Catholic schools provided education to a number of the leading *philosophes,* they were unable to form a philosopher who could defend official doctrine against new irreligious currents. Catholic authors who wrote on the heresies were neither intelligent nor talented enough to refute convincingly the menacing philosophy emanating from the *salons*. Jean Hermant's *Histoire des hérésies*, a very popular book (four editions in seven years), has an expanded index and that is all that can be said in its favor. Hermant, it is true, resorted to a new interpretation when he spoke of Wyclyf but his invasion of the field of speculation is unfortunate. Even at this late date he worked more with suppositions than with facts. Alluding to the *Responsio* of 1377 Hermant wrote: "Wiclef attaqua d'abord le dénier de Saint Pierre que les Papes levoient en Angleterre depuis Innocent III . . . ."[79] John Ball was again made an associate of Wyclyf (*prêtre Wiclefiste*) and leader of the uprising during which peasants yelled *Liberté*.[80] Wyclyf did not take part in the Rebellion but in Hermant's view he was the spark which started the conflagration—the Grey Eminence of the movement:

> Comme Wiclef ne s'étoit point trouvé ni dans les Assemblées des Séditieux, ni à l'assassinat de l'Archevêque, soit qu'il ne fut pas alors tourmenté de la passion de lui succéder, ou qu'il s'en fut démis volontairement en faveur de Ballée [John Ball], ou que sa timidité naturelle fut devenuë dans son esprit plus forte que l'ambition, il laissa aux autres courir tout le danger de l'entreprise, lorqu'il attendoit en lieu sûr quel en seroit le succès.[81]

Then came his retirement to Wales, a mistake which proves that Varillas had at least one follower, and the paralytical stroke on 29 December 1384 when he wanted to preach against—echoing Walsingham—St. Thomas of Canterbury. The death which comes correctly on 31 December 1384 is not only a deliverance to Wyclyf but to the reader also.[82]

Hermant was not the only writer of the time who tried to expose the errors of the heretics. F. A. A. Pluquet published two volumes in 1762 called *Mémoires pour servir à l'histoire des égarements de l'esprit humain par rapport à la religion chrétienne,* a title meant to attract many an inquisitive mind by its scholarly wording. However, the appearance is deceptive, and the reality disappointing. Pluquet distorted facts like Hermant without indulging in dramatization of events. He preferred to generalize: "Le Clergé d'Angleterre avait toujours pris le parti des papes contre les rois & contre le parlement, il avoit retenu le peuple dans la fidélité au saint Siége."[83] This did not prevent him from claiming, after he has discussed various articles of Wyclyf's heretical creed (real presence, dominion dependent on grace, and others) that "Les ouvrages de Wiclef contenaient donc des principes assortis aux différens caractères, proportionnés aux différentes sortes d'esprit, & favorables à l'indisposition assez générale en Angleterre contre le pape, contre le clergé, contre les Moines: *on conçoit donc qu'il se fît des disciples* [italics added]."[84] The latter part of the sentence, one feels, is an observation reflecting eighteenth-century French political and social conditions applied to the times of Wyclyf despite the fact that it contradicts Pluquet's earlier assertion.

Pluquet knew that Wyclyf's idea of dominion was based on grace. He equally knew that Wyclyf believed man loses the right to his posses- sions once he commits a mortal sin. Pluquet thought he could reinter- pret Wyclyf's proposition in favor of the clergy. He did so in the first part of the reconstruction but finished on a note resembling the codicil that destroys the testament:

> Il est étonnant que Wiclef, qui n'avançait cette maxime que pour autoriser les fidèles à dépouiller le clergé de ses richesses, n'ait pas vu qu'elle éta- blissait le clergé maître absolu de tous les biens temporels, puisqu'il n'appartient en effet qu'à l'Église de juger si un homme est coupable d'un péché mortel; car abandonner ce jugement aux particuliers, comme Wiclef le faisait, c'était ouvrir la porte à tous les vols & à toutes les guerres. Les fureurs des Hussites & des Anabaptistes qui désolèrent l'Allemagne après Wiclef, sont les effets de cette doctrine.[85]

With this example of logic fresh in the mind let us examine the last Catholic writer under review, namely Father Peter Maria Grassi, an Italian from Vicenza. It must be said immediately that Grassi chose the *via bona* of following Thomas Netter of Walden and Walsingham, and avoided dangerous speculations which led the other two Catholic heresiologists into pits full of errors. Grassi presented cogent argu- ments for the continued justification of the condemnation of Wyclyf, and for the perpetuation of the view that he was a heretic. In fact, Grassi said that Wyclyf was "de nostri temporis Haereticorum Pro- toparens."[86] Grassi did not here invent any heresy. He meant the *colluvies* which snatched Northern Europe from the Catholic world. Grassi's narrative has a comprehensive selection of essential events which are never colored by the brush of fantasy. The author opened new views only where he felt there was space for them and where he might tread safely. He probed the riddle of the beginning of Wyclyf's public career, and selected (after scrutinizing fifteen different dates from 1352 to 1397) 1352, first advanced by Prateolus (Gabriel Du Préau).[87] Nor was that the only miscalculation he made. He also at- tempted to cut the Gordian knot entwined by the two strands of the heretics who appeared, as he could read in Walsingham, after Wyclyf's death: the Lollards and the Wyclyfites. He first rejected the notion that they originated from the semi-mystical heretic Walter Lollard; identifying the Wyclyfites with the Lollards, he derived their name from Arundel and the Latin "lolium."[88] Grassi also revived the old scene between the ailing Wyclyf and the friars eager to see him dead.[89] Thus we see he had read Foxe. The Augustinian monk considered it his duty to defend St. Augustine against Wyclyf's impudent words that the latter and Augustine agreed on many doctrinal subjects. After noting that Wyclyf's imposture had been exploded by Netter, Grassi had no more to say.[90]

Among Protestants of lesser renown we do not meet such a unanimity of opinion concerning Wyclyf as among the Catholics. William Gilpin started the trend of writing the biographies of Wyclyf sympathetically but without sufficient research. Gilpin wrote with the help of John Lewis. He is, however, more verbose and, moreover, thoroughly imbued with the spirit of traditionalism: "The writings of the schoolmen, [Wyclyf] soon found, were calculated only to make sectaries; the Bible alone to make a rational Christian."[91] Archbishop Courtenay was called "an inflamed bigot."[92] Being a churchman and a teacher, he found no sympathy for John Ball, "a conceited, empty fellow, who, through motives of vanity, was ready to adopt any singularity."[93] On the other hand, to Wyclyf he allows noble attributes, and the glories of Gilpin's age are transferred to Wyclyf in this apotheosis:

> His amazing penetration; his rational manner of thinking; and the noble freedom of his spirit, are equally the objects of our admiration. Wicliff was in religion, what Bacon was afterwards in science; the great detecter of those arts and glosses, which the barbarism of ages had drawn together to obscure the mind of man.[94]

Henry Carr was of the same opinion although his language is reminiscent more of the passionate debates of the older past than the cold reasoning of the eighteenth century. His title, *The History of Popery: With such Alterations of Phrase, as may be more Suitable to the Taste of this Age; . . .* is deceptive. Wyclyf, compared to Hercules because he cleaned the Augean stables of his time, is seen in high notes of admiration. All the accusations made by the Catholics are rejected. Did Wyclyf want the bishopric of Worcester? No! "This is only the malicious Suggestion of *Parsons* and *Brerely,* and such upstart Pettifoggers for the Church of *Rome*: . . . . It must be remembered, that Wickliff lived in a most corrupt Age, when the Clergy where [sic] so seared in Impiety, that it required sharp Launcings, and good store of Vinegar to make them sensible."[95] This was the offered explanation of Wyclyf's belief that no bishop is a bishop while in a state of mortal sin. That Wyclyf was undoubtedly under God's protection is illustrated by a story, fully accepted in the rationalist era: "A Child finding one of *Wickliff*'s Bones which in haste was left or forgotten, running with it to carry to the rest in the Bonefire [*sic*], brake his Leg. Here was *Lex Talionis, Bone for Bone.*"[96]

The diversity of views in the eighteenth century is not better illustrated than by an exactly different opinion which appeared in a book called *Historical Collections Relating to Remarkable Periods of the Success of the Gospel, and Eminent Instruments Employed in Promoting it.* John Gillies, who assembled from passages by different authors a short encyclopaedia of religion, evidently found pleasure in the words of Richard Field, a divine of the seventeenth century, and he repeats them in 1755: "Altho' we do acknowledge Wickliff, Husse, Jerom of Prague, &c. to have been worthy servants of God, and holy martyrs, suffering for the cause of Christ against Antichrist, yet we do not think that the church was to be found only in them . . . ."[97]

The last representative of this gallery of secondary writers on Wyclyf is a *Weltpriester* from Bohemia. His account embodies the watchwords of progressive intellectuals of the times, combined with the pride that Wyclyf was really a *Landsmann* of the Czechs.[98] Augustin Zitte's work provides interesting corroboration for the swift spread of ideas among eighteenth-century intellectuals, and the distribution of historical literature. He frankly acknowledged that he closely followed William Gilpin.[99] He should have known, from the footnotes in Gilpin, that John Lewis had published a superior work on Wyclyf earlier in the same century, but oddly does not show any knowledge of Lewis. He does not compare, but relies on the more modern work, adding only here and there a new stylistic expression or a new, strong word. This course, however, led Zitte into difficult straits. He read in Zedler's *Das allgemeine grosse Historische Lexicon* that Wyclyf received from the king (or rather was confirmed in) the prebend of Aust. He refused to believe it, not because the question of plurality haunted his conscience, but because the "zuverlässigsten englischen Skribenten von dem angeführten Kanonikate zu Aust gar Keine Meldung thun."[100] Zitte was convinced of Wyclyf's moral integrity. The story concerning the bishopric of Worcester made him remark that Wyclyf could never have requested it, "weil dieses Verlangen em wahres Pasquill auf seine Lehren gewesen wäre."[101] Zitte made an interesting point for the time when writing of the Lollards and Wyclyfites: he thought that they were distinct and separate sects; the latter embracing Wyclyf's teaching as a whole, the former only his social and ecclesiastical views.[102] This opinion was not taken up by any writer of importance, and lost itself among the less accurate characteristics of the book, among which the designation of Loughborough as Wyclyf's place of birth is only one, but certainly the most blatant.[103]

This striking diversity of opinions, and its damaging influence on historical literature did not pass unnoticed, and no one wrote about it more eloquently and perceptively than the Swiss Johann Conrad Füessli. Although on the historical plane he presented conclusions which cannot now nor could then be supported with evidence—except very circumstantially—on the theoretical level his arguments on the nature of historical writing do not lack perspicacity.[104] He speaks of the "affekten der Menschen" which endanger history, he demurs to the way how especially the history of the heretics is written, and being convinced that his loyalty is only to truth and impartiality, he delivers this message:

> Viele tractiren diese Geschichte mit Heftigkeit. Die Protestanten widerlegen die Katholischen Scribenten: dann tretten von dieser Partey andere auf und widerlegen die ersten dagegen. Die neurn Scribenten erklären die alten, der eine so, der andere anderst. Laraus entstehet nichts, als Zank und Streit, Der Historie ist aber doch nicht geholfen; vielmehr ist sie auf diese Weise verworren gemacht worden.[105]

The historical literature of the nineteenth century unfortunately proves history has not set itself free from this vicious circle.

The fragmentation of intellectual thought begun in the eighteenth century was an accomplished fact in the nineteen hundreds. Living too close to the period beginning with the "dancing" Congress of Vienna and ending with the blood-stained streets of Sarajevo and Petersburg, we often lack the proper perspective to gauge the significance of the change which then occurred, whose influence still affects us. Even such a minor field of investigation as the history of Wyclyf bears the marks of the transformation of the traditional opinions and judgments, and is treated *de novo* on many different levels. This development cannot be entirely divorced from what Elie Halévy called the acceleration of history; we may only add that while Halévy had in mind only historical events we enlarge his meaning to include the rise of an increasingly larger production of historical works written under different viewpoints. Moreover, the emergence of the new literature and the cavalier treatment accorded to the old accounts indicate that not only facts but also historical works are unique, and never repeat themselves once the environment changes and assumes new forms of expression. And it would be useless to deny, should an attempt be made to determine the long-range development of world history, that the development of human society moves from a God-centered to a Man-centered universe.

This retreat from religion as the world-view of the Western man may be detected in the works on Wyclyf which appeared in the nineteenth and twentieth centuries. Their authors are more concerned with the elucidation of "irreducible and stubborn facts" than with the age-old controversy of the past whether Wyclyf was a tool of God or an instrument of the Devil. Historians of the time tried to make the canon of *wie es eigentlich gewesen* overcome their personal sympathies, and the accounts offered to the public by those writers who presented Wyclyf in older idioms were condemned to oblivion.

Twenty-four years before the foundation of the Wyclif Society, Walter Waddington Shirley, D.D., Canon of Christ Church and Regius Professor of Ecclesiastical History in Oxford, edited the *Fasciculi Zizaniorum* for the Rolls Series. His scholarly introduction is free of verbose adjectives. Shirley contented himself with the known statement: "To the memory of one of the greatest of Englishmen his country has been singularly and painfully ungrateful . . . —he is the first of the reformers."[106] The same restraint was not exercised by J. Jackson Wray in 1884. In his biography of Wyclyf dedicated to the "Common People," the fourteenth-century reformer is hailed as "a palm-tree in the desert, a cedar of Lebanon among brushwood, a freeman amid a race of slaves."[107] Today, while Shirley is still remembered, Wray's name is forgotten. The reason for this lies in the intellectual revolution of the nineteenth century. The establishment of reliable methodology meant the appearance of historian-scientists. And once professional historians appeared on the scene they evolved their own postulates, and these separated them from the people at large; and the work they accomplished redounded mostly to the benefit of their own caste. On the other hand, Wray's failure may be ascribed to the secularization of society, a society which regards the great religious issues of the past as outmoded and irrelevant to present-day affairs. The new approach to the old historical problems affected even the church historians; divine elements disappeared from history together with the authors's religious convictions, and the great problem—whether Wyclyf was right or wrong in attacking the Church—was left suspended in the air like an interrogation mark to which there is no immediate answer.

Notes

[1] Louis Moréri, *Le Grand Dictionnaire Historique,* was first published in 1674 in Lyon ninety-seven years before the first edition of the *Encyclopaedia Britannica.* In 1758 appeared its twentieth edition.
[2] L. Ellies-Dupin, *Nouvelle bibliothèque des auteurs ecclésiastiques,* . . . , 2nd ed., 19 vols. (Paris, 1693–1715), I, Preface p. 9.

[3] *Ibid.*, I, 13.

[4] *Ibid.*, XII, 128.

[5] *Idem.*

[6] *Idem.*

[7] *Ibid.*, XII, 130. See John Stow, *The Annales of England* (London, 1631), 296, and Anthony à Wood, *Historia et Antiquitates Universitatis Oxoniensis,* 2 vols. (Oxford, 1674), I, 193. Stow conceived of history in the following words: ''The Law of God forbiddeth us to receive a false report and the law of *Histories* is, that we ought to publish no falshood, nor dissemble any truth.'' *Ibid.*, sign. a 2 r.

[8] Ellies-Dupin, *Nouvelle bibliothèque,* XII, 130.

[9] *Idem.*

[10] *Ibid.*, XII, 131. Ortuinus Gratius is the compiler of *Fasciculus rerum expetendarum ac fugiendarum,* a collection of documents bearing on the Middle Ages. The first edition appeared in Cologne in 1535. The valuable work was re-edited by Edward Brown in London in 1690. Ortuinus was known to Rabelais, who ascribed to him the work *Ars honeste petandi in societate,* a work which Pantagruel found in the Library of St. Victor. Rabelais, *Gargantua et Pantagruel,* ed. Louis Moland, ''Classiques Garnier,'' 2 vols. (Paris: Garnier, 1956), I, 180; II, 488. The Glossary explains in Rabelaisian terms the strange title of the work supposedly written by Ortuinus Gratius. The *Fasciculus* contains *Tractatus contra errores Wiclefi in Trialogo* of William Woodford. In Brown's edition, pp. 190–265.

[11] Ellies-Dupin, *Nouvelle bibliothèque,* XI sign. * 2 r.

[12] Claude Fleury, *Histoire ecclésiastique,* new ed., 36 vols. (Paris, 1742).

[13] *Ibid.*, XX, 268. ''Ecclesiasticus, immo et Romanus pontifex, potest legitime a subditis et laicis corripi, et etiam accusari.''

[14] *Idem.* ''Viclef donna une explication sur ces dix-neuf propositions, ou sans en retracter aucune, il s'efforce de les justifier par des subtilités scholastiques, aussie obscures la plupart que les propositions mêmes. Il insiste beaucoup sur le domaine temporel & sur les excommunications qu'il s'efforce d'affoiblir.''

[15] *Ibid.*, p. 368.

[16] *Ibid.*, p. 311.

[17] *Ibid.*, p. 312.

[18] *Idem.*

[19] *Ibid.*, p. 369.

[20] Gottfried Arnold, *Unpartheyische Kirchen- und Ketzer-Historie, von Anfang des Neuen Testaments biss auf das Jahr Christi 1688,* 2 vols. (Frankfurt, 1729). The first edition appeared in 1699. Arnold proclaimed at the very outset of his *History* that he would not use as his authorities ''babblers, hypocrites and braggarts.'' *Ibid.*, I, 4.

[21] *Ibid.*, I, 16.

[22] *Ibid.*, I, 427.

[23] *Ibid.*, I, 428.

[24] *Idem.*

[25] *Idem.*

[26] Pierre Bayle, *Dictionnaire historique et critique,* new ed., 16 vols. (Paris, 1820–24). The first edition appeared in 1695–97 and was followed in 1702 by a second one.

[27] *Ibid.*, XIV, 564.

[28] Matthias Earbery, *The Pretended Reformers: Or, The History of the Heresie of John Wickliffe, John Huss, and Jerom of Prague* (London, 1717), p. vi.

[29] *Idem.*

[30] *Ibid.*, p. vii.

[31] *Ibid.*, pp. vii–ix.

[32] *Ibid.*, p. ix.

[33] *Ibid.*, p. iii.

[34] John Lewis, *The History of the Life and Suffering of the Reverend and Learned John Wicliffe, D.D.* (London, 1720). I have used the second edition of 1723 which is textually unchanged.

[35] Ibid., p. xvii.

[36] Ibid., pp. iii, xii.

[37] Ibid., pp. 2–3, 14, 30–34, 43, 81–101 and ff.

[38] Ibid., pp. 3, 5.

[39] Ibid., p. 52.

[40] Ibid., pp. 50–63.

[41] Ibid., p. 1.

[42] Ibid., p. v.

[43] William Cave, Scriptorum ecclesiasticorum Historia Literaria, with Appendix contributed by Henry Wharton and Robert Gerius, new ed., 2 vols. (Basel, 1741–45; Appendix is dated 1743), II, App. 62. The first edition appeared in 1688–89; the second was published in 1720.

[44] Ibid., p. 63.

[45] Idem.

[46] Ibid., p. 64.

[47] Thomas Tanner, Bibliotheca Britannico-Hibernica (London, 1748), p. 767.

[48] "Wicliff, John," Biographia Britannica, 1766, Vol. VI, Part ii, 4260–2. We are told in this same article that Wyclyf went as ambassador to Milan. This information is based—as the marginal note indicates—on "MS Twyne 246." I have searched the Twyne MSS. in the Bodleian but have been unable to discover the information in the many notes left behind by Twyne. This writer of the seventeenth century considered Wyclyf "the very maine pillar of our church as all the world knoweth." Bodleian, MS., Wood D. 32 [S.C. 25208] fol. 139 r. new pagination 6a.

[49] Biographia Britannica, VI, part ii, 4262. Bigots were those who sent the nineteen articles to pope Gregory XI. Ibid., VI, ii, 4260.

[50] Ibid., VI, ii, 4262, note qq.; 4266.

[51] Louis Moréri, Le Grand Dictionnaire Historique, où le Mélange curieux de l'histoire sacrée et profane, . . . ed. Drouet, rev. ed. (Paris, 1759), X, 806.

[52] The author of the article relied on Lewis's work on Wyclyf and drew much of its factual knowledge from it. The less accurate statements he borrowed from Louis Maimbourg, Histoire du grand schisme d'Occident, 2nd ed., 2 vols. (Paris, 1686).

[53] "Wiclef. (Johann)," Grosses vollstaendiges Universal Lexicon aller Wissenschaften und Kuenste, 64 vols. (Leipzig and Halle, 1732–54), LV, cols. 1711–31.

[54] Ibid., I, dedication.

[55] Ibid., LV, col. 1711. "Wiclef, . . . ein Doctor der Theologie im 14 Jahrhunderte, wird von den Catholischen unter die Ketzer, von den Protestanten aber unter die unerschrockenen Bekenner der Wahrheit in Engelland gesetzet."

[56] Ibid., LV, col. 1731. Who has ever heard of Hartknoch and Loeder?

[57] Ibid., LV, cols. 1723 ff.

[58] Idem.

[59] Zedler went only as far as to admit that "Man kan auch nicht laeugnen, dass Wiclef unbestaendig in seinen Meyungen gewesen . . . ." Ibid., LV, col. 1722.

[60] Voltaire, Essai sur les moeurs, 3 vols. (Paris: Garnier, 1878), I, 427. [The section deals with the Hohenstaufen emperor, Frederick II.]

[61] Ibid., II, 1.

[62] Ibid., II, 2.

[63] Idem.

[64] Idem.

[65] Ibid., II, 2–3.

[66] David Hume, The History of England from the Invasion of Julius Caesar to the Revolution in 1688, 5 vols. (London: Bowyer, 1806), I, v–vi.

[67] Letter of Adam Smith to William Strahan, ibid., I, xiii.

[68] David Hume, The History of England from the Invasion of Julius Caesar to the Accession of Henry VII, 2 vols. (London: Millar, 1762), II, 276.

[69] *Idem.*

[70] *Ibid.*, II, 276–279 *passim.*

[71] *Ibid.*, II, 277.

[72] *Idem.*

[73] *Idem.*

[74] *Ibid.*, II, 278.

[75] *Ibid.*, II, 277.

[76] *Ibid.*, II, 279.

[77] Condorcet, "Esquisse d'un tableau historique des progrès de l'esprit humain," *Oeuvres,* eds. A. Condorcet O'Connor and M. F. Arago, 12 vols. (Paris: Firmin Didot, 1847–49), VI, 131–132.

[78] *Ibid.*, VI, 131. ". . . le peuple parut vouloir ressaisir ses véritables droits . . . ."

[79] Jean Hermant, *Histoire des Hérésies* . . . , 3rd. ed., 4 vols. (Rouen, 1727), IV, 406.

[80] *Ibid.*, IV, 412–413.

[81] *Ibid.*, IV, 413.

[82] *Ibid.*, IV, 418–420.

[83] F. A. A. Pluquet, *Mémoires pour servir à l'histoire des égaremens de l'esprit humain par rapport à la religion chrétienne; ou dictionnaire des hérésies, des erreurs et des schismes; . . . ,* 2 vols. (Paris, 1762), II, 637. [It has been necessary to confirm the Pluquet quotations from the nouvelle édition, 1845. The three citations will be found in II (1845), 605, 611, 609, respectively.]

[84] *Ibid.*, II, 644–645.

[85] *Ibid.*, II, 642.

[86] Petrus Maria Grassi, *De Ortu ac Progressu Haeresum Io. Witclefi in Anglia Presbyteri Narratio Historica* (Vicentiae, 1707), *epistola dedicatoria.*

[87] *Ibid.*, p. 20.

[88] *Ibid.*, pp. 65–69.

[89] *Ibid.*, p. 140.

[90] *Ibid.*, p. 385 ff.

[91] William Gilpin, *The Life of John Wyclif,* "Select Biography," Vol. II (London: Wetton and Jarvis, 1821), p. 4.

[92] *Ibid.*, p. 21.

[93] *Ibid.*, p. 39.

[94] *Ibid.*, p. 49.

[95] Henry Carr, *The History of Popery: With such Alterations of Phrase, as may be more Suitable to the Taste of this Age; . . . ,* 2 vols. (London, 1735–36), II, 165–166.

[96] *Ibid.*, II, 170.

[97] John Gillies, *Historical Collections Relating to Remarkable Periods of the Success of the Gospel, and Eminent Instruments Employed in Promoting it,* 2 vols. (Glasgow, 1754), I, 35.

[98] Augustin Zitte, *Lebensbeschreibung des Englischen Reformators Johannes Wiklef* (Prague, 1786), p. 4.

[99] *Ibid.*, p. 87.

[100] *Ibid.*, p. 114.

[101] *Ibid.*, p. 111.

[102] *Ibid.*, p. 80.

[103] *Ibid.*, p. 113.

[104] Johann Conrad Füessli, *Neue und unpartheyische Kirchen- und Ketzer-historie der mittlern Zeit,* 3 vols. (Frankfurt, 1770–4), I, 3–4. In Füessli's opinion the Lollards existed before Wyclyf and "they woke him up." The Lollards in turn derived their teaching from the Valdensians. *Ibid.*, II, 32.

[105] *Ibid.*, II, 162–3.

[106] W. W. Shirley, ed., *Fasciculi Zizaniorum Magistri Johannis Wyclif cum Tritico* (London, 1858), p. xlvi. [Shirley edited less than half the Bodleian Library MS. for the

Rolls Series. A survey of the contents of the MS., suggestions of provenance, and the likelihood of Thomas Netter of Walden as author are discussed in James Crompton, "Fasciculi Zizaniorum," *Journal of Ecclesiastical History,* XII (1962), 35–45, 155–66.]

[107] J. Jackson Wray, *John Wycliffe: A Quincentenary Tribute* (London: Nisbet, 1884), p. 57. In the same year in a work as unknown as that of Wray, John Wilson wrote that Wyclyf's early "daily teachers" would be "woods and rills, the silence that is in the starry sky, the sleep that is among the lonely hills . . . ." J. L. Wilson, *John Wycliffe, Patriot and Reformer, "The Morning Star of the Reformation"* (New York: Funk and Wagnalls, 1884), p. 19.

Bibliography of Materials Cited

Abbot, Robert. *A Mirrour of Popish Subtilties*. London, 1594.

Adam, Daniel, of Veleslavín. *Kalendar Hystorycky*. 2nd ed. Prague, 1590.

Aeneas Sylvius Piccolomini. *Opera quae extant omnia*. Balileae, 1579.

Arnold, Gottfreid. *Unpartheyische Kirchen- und Ketzer-Historie, von Anfang des Neuen Testaments biss auf das Jahr Christi 1688*. 2 vols. Frankfurt, 1729.

Aston, M. E. "John Wycliffe's Reformation Reputation," *Past and Present*, Number 30 (1965), 23–51.

———. "Lollardy and Sedition, 1381–1431," *Past and Present*, Number 17 (1960), 1–44.

———. "Lollardy and the Reformation: Survival or Revival?," *History*, XLIX (1964), 149–70.

Bainton, Roland H. *Here I Stand, A Life of Martin Luther*. New York: Mentor-The New American Library, 1955.

Balbin, Bohuslav. *Epitome historica rerum bohemicarum*. Prague, 1677.

———. *Rozprava na obranu jazyka slovanskeho, zvlaste pak ceskeho*. (Dissertatio apologetica pro lingua slavonica praecipue bohemica.) Translated from the Latin by Emanuel Tonner. Praha: Spolek pro vydavani lacinych knih ceskych, 1869.

Bale, John. *Scriptorum illustrium maioris Brytannie, quam nunc Angliam & Scotiam vocant: Catalogus*. Basileae, 1557.

———. *Scriptorum illustrium maioris Brytanniae posterior pars, quinque continens centurias ultimas*. Basileae, 1559.

———. *Illustrium maioris Britanniae scriptorum, hoc est, Angliae, Cambriae, ac Scotiae summarium in quasdam centurias divisum*. Ipswich, 1548.

Barnes, Joshua. *The History of that Most Victorious Monarch Edward III^d, King of England and France and Lord of Ireland, And First Founder of the Most Noble Order of the Garter*. Cambridge, 1688.

Bartoš, F. M. *Literární činnost M. J. Husi*. Praha: Ceska Akademie ved a umeni, 1948.

Baxter, Richard. *Church-History of the Government of Bishops and their Councils Abbreviated*. London, 1680.

Bayle, Pierre. *Dictionnaire historique et critique*. New ed., 16 vols. Paris, 1820–4.

Bellarmin, Robert Cardinal. *De Controversiis christianae fidei, adversus huius temporis haereticos*. Rev. ed., 4 vols. Ingolstadii, 1601.

———. *De Scriptoribus Ecclesiasticis Liber unus*. Coloniae, 1684.

Belle-Forest, François de. *Les Grandes annales, et histoire generale de France, des le reyne de Philippe de Valois, iusques à Henri III, a present heureusement regnant*. Vol. II. Paris, 1579.

Benrath, G. A. "Wyclif und Hus," *Zeitschrift für Theologie und Kirche*, LXII (1965), 196–216.

Benthem, Henrich Ludolff. *Engländischer Kirch- und Schulen-Staat*. Lüneburg, 1694.

Bernardus de Lutzenburgo. *Catalogus Haereticorum*. Coloniae, 1522; 2nd ed., Coloniae, 1523; 5th ed., Coloniae, 1537.

Bèze, Théodore de. *Les vrais pourtraits des hommes illustres en piété et doctrine . . . .* Translated by Simon Goulart. Génève, 1581.

Bettenson, Henry, ed. *Documents of the Christian Church*. London: Oxford University Press, 1943.

Betts, R. R. *Essays in Czech History*. London: Athlone Press, 1969.

Biographia Britannica. "John Wicliff." London, 1766. VI, part II, 4257–66.

Bossuet, Jacques-Bénigne. *Histoire des variations des Églises protestantes*. 6th ed., 2 vols. Paris, 1718.

Brandt, Miroslav. "Wyclifitism in Dalmatia in 1383," *Slavonic and East European Review*, XXXVI (1957–8), 58–68.

British Library, Lansdowne MS. 446.

Brock, Peter. *Political and Social Doctrines of the Unity of Czech Brethren in the Fifteenth and Early Sixteenth Centuries.* The Hague: Mouton, 1957.

Brown, David. "Wiclif and Hus," *British and Foreign Evangelical Review,* XXXIII (1884), 572–8.

Burnet, Gilbert. *The History of the Reformation of the Church of England.* 7 vols. Oxford: Oxford University Press, 1829.

————. *Reflections on Mr. Varillas's History of the Revolutions that have happned [sic] in Europe in matters of Religion. And more particularly on his ninth book that relates to England.* Amsterdam, 1686.

————. *Reflections on Mr. Varillas's History of the Revolutions that have hapned [sic] in Europe in matters of Religion. And more particularly on his ninth book that relates to England.* London, 1689.

————. *A Letter to Mr. Thevenot. Containing a censure of Mr. La Grand's History of King Henry the Eighth's Divorce. To which is added, a Censure of Mr. de Meaux's History of the Variations of the Protestant Churches. Together with some further reflections on Mr. Le Grand.* London, 1689.

————. *A Continuation of Reflections of Mr. Varillas's History of Heresies. Particularly on that which relates to English affairs. In his third and fourth tomes.* Amsterdam, 1687.

————. *A Defence of the Reflections on the ninth book of the first volum [sic] of Mr. Varillas's History of Heresies. Being a reply to his Answer.* Amsterdam, 1687.

Bzovius, Abraham. *Historiae ecclesiasticae.* 18 vols. Coloniae Agrippinae, 1617–27.

Cano, Francisco Melchor. "De locis theologicis libri duodecim" and "Relectio de Poenitentiae Sacramento" in *Opera.* Ed. R. Vadilaus. Coloniae Agrippinae, 1605.

Carr, Henry. *The History of Popery: With such Alterations of Phrase, as may be more suitable to the Taste of this Age; and such Additions, as may improve the History, Strengthen the Argument, and better accomodate it to the present State of Popery in Great Britain.* 2 vols. London, 1735–6.

Castro Zamorense, Alphonsus à. *Adversus omnes haereses libri quatuordecim.* Parisiis, 1571.

Catharinus, Ambrosius. *Speculum Haereticorum.* Cracoviae, 1540.

Cave, William. *Scriptorum ecclesiasticorum Historia Literaria.* (Appendix contributed by Henry Wharton and Robert Gerius.) New ed., 2 vols. Basel: Johann Rudolf Imhoff, 1741–5.

Cellarius, Christophorus. *Historia medii aevi a temporibus Constantini Magni ad Constantinopolim a Turcis captam deducta, et cum notis perpetuis ac tabulis synopticis iterum edita.* Jena, 1698.

Chelčický, Petr. *Sit Viry.* [*The Net of Faith.*] Ed. Emil Smetanka. Prague: Comenium, 1912.

Chronicon Henrici Knighton vel Cnitthon, Monachis Leycestrensis. Ed. J. R. Lumby. 2 vols. London: "Rolls Series," 1889–95.

Clarke, Samuel. *A Generall Martyrologie, containing a collection of all the greatest persecutions which have befallen the Church of Christ from the Creation to our present times. Whereunto are added, the Lives of sundry modern Divines.* London, 1651.

Cochlaeus, K. Dobneck (J.). *Historiae Hussitarum libri duodecim.* Apud S. Victorem prope Moguntiam, 1549.

————. *Warhafftige Historia von Magister Johan Hussen von anfang seiner newen Sect bisz zum ende seines lebens ym Concilio zu Costnitz aufs alten Originaln beschrieben.* Leipzig, 1537.

Coleridge, Samuel Taylor. *Literary Remains.* 4 vols. London: W. Pickering, 1836–9.

Condorcet, Jacques Marie de Caritat de. *Oeuvres.* Ed. A. C. O'Connor and M. F. Arago. 12 vols. Paris: Firmin Didot, 1847–9.

Cook, W. R. "John Wyclif and Hussite Theology, 1415–1436," *Church History,* XLII (1973), 335–49.

Cooper, Thompson. "John Lewis," *Dictionary of National Biography,* XI (1909), 1065.

Coussord, Claudius. *Valdensium ac quorundam aliorum errores, praecipuas, ac pene omnes, quae nunc vigent, haereseis continentes.* Parisiis, 1548.

Cox, Francis Augustus. *The Life of Philip Melancthon.* 2nd ed. rev. London: Gale, Fenner, 1817.

Crespin, Jean. *Recueil de plusieurs personnes qui ont constamment enduré la mort pour le nom de nostre Seigneur Iesus Christ, depuis Iean Wicleff, & Iean Hus iusques à ceste année presente M.D.LV.* Geneva, 1555.

———. *La vie de M. Iean Wicleff.* Lyon, 1565.

Crompton, James. "Fasciculi Zizaniorum," *Journal of Ecclesiastical History,* XII (1962), 35–45, 155–66.

———. "John Wyclif: A Study in Mythology," *Transactions of the Leicestershire Archaeological and Historical Society,* XLII (1966–7), 6–34.

Dahmus, J. H. "Further Evidence for the Spelling 'Wyclyf'," *Speculum,* XVI (1941), 224.

———. "John Wyclif and the English Government," *Speculum,* XXXV (1960), 51–68.

Daly, L. J. *The Political Theory of John Wyclif.* Chicago: Loyola University Press, 1962.

de Boor, Friedrich. *Wyclifs Simoniebegriff. Die theologischen und kirchenpolitischen Grundlagen der Kirchenkritik John Wyclifs.* Halle: Niemeyer, 1970.

Denzinger, Henricus. *Enchiridion Symbolorum Definitionum et Declarationum de Rebus Fidei et Morum.* Ed. Carolus Rahner, S.J. 30th ed. Freiburg: Herder, 1955.

de Vooght, Paul. *L'hérésie de Jean Huss.* 2nd rev. ed., 2 vols. Louvain: Publications Universitaires de Louvain, 1975.

Dubravius, J. *Historiae regni Boiemiae.* Prostannae, 1552.

Prateolus (Du Préau), Gabriel. *De vitis, sectis, et dogmatibus omnium haereticorum qui ab orbe condito, ad nostra usque tempora, & veterum & recentium authorum monimentis proditi sunt, elenchus alphabeticus.* Coloniae, 1569.

———. *Histoire de l'estat et succès de l'Église, dressée en forme de chronique générale et universelle . . . depuis la nativité de Jésus-Christ jusques en l'an 1580 . . . .* 12 vols. Paris, 1583.

Earbery, Matthias. *The Pretended Reformers: Or, The History of the Heresie of John Wickliffe, John Huss, and Jerom of Prague.* London, 1717.

Ekwall, Eilert. *The Concise Oxford Dictionary of English Place-names.* Oxford: Clarendon Press, 1936.

Ellies-Dupin, Louis. *Nouvelle bibliothèque des auteurs ecclésiastiques.* 2nd ed., 14 vols. Paris, 1690–1713.

Emden, A. B. *A Biographical Register of the University of Oxford to A.D. 1500.* 3 vols. Oxford: Clarendon Press, 1957–9.

Eymericus, Nicolaus. *Directorium Inquisitorum, cum commentariis Francisci Pegnae.* Rev. and enl. ed.; Romae, 1585.

Fabri, Johann. *Wie sich Johannis Huszs, der Pickarder, und Johannis von Wessalia Leren und Buecher mit Martino Luther vergleichen.* Leipzig, 1528.

Fasciculi Zizaniorum Magistri Johannis Wyclif cum Tritico. Ed. W. W. Shirley. London: "Rolls Series," 1858.

Figgis, J. N. "John Wyclif" in *Typical English Churchmen.* Series II. The Church Historical Society, LXXVIII. London: Society for the Promotion of Christian Knowledge, 1909.

Flathe, J. L. F. *Geschichte der Vorläufer der Reformation.* 2 vols. Leipzig: Goeschen, 1835–6.

Fleury, Claude. *Histoire ecclésiastique.* New ed., 36 vols. Paris, 1758–61.

Fosdick, Harry Emerson, ed. *Great Voices of the Reformation.* New York: The Modern Library, 1952.

Fox, Levi, ed. *English Historical Scholarship in the Sixteenth and Seventeenth Centuries.* Published for the Dugdale Society by the Oxford University Press, 1956.

Foxe, John. *Actes and monuments of these latter and perillous dayes, touching matters of the Church . . . .* London: John Day, 1563.

————. *Actes and monuments of matters most speciall and memorable, happenyng in the Church, with an universall history of the same*. 4th ed., 2 vols. London, 1583.

————. *The First Volume of the Ecclesiasticall History, Contayning the Actes and Monumentes of Thinges Passed in Every Kinges Time in this Realme, especially in the Church of England*. London: John Daye, 1576.

Füessli, Johann Conrad. *Neue und unpartheyische Kirchen- und Ketzer-historie der mittlern Zeit*. 3 vols. Frankfurt, 1770–4.

Fuller, Thomas. *Abel Redevivus: Or, The Dead yet Speaking, The Lives and Deaths of the Moderne Divines*. London, 1651.

————. *The Church History of Britain: From the Birth of Jesus Christ untill the Year MDCXLVIII*. London, 1655.

————. *The Worthies of England*. Ed. John Freeman. London: Allen and Unwin, 1952 [1662].

Gascoigne, Thomas. *Loci e libro veritatum*. Ed. J. E. T. Rogers. Oxford: Clarendon Press, 1881.

Gesner, Conrad. *Bibliotheca Universalis, sive Catalogus omnium scriptorum locupletissimus*. Tiguri, 1545.

Gierke, Otto. *Political Theories of the Middle Age*. Trans. and intr. F. W. Maitland. Boston: Beacon Press, 1958.

Gillies, John. *Historical Collections Relating to Remarkable Periods of the Success of the Gospel, and Eminent Instruments Employed in Promoting it*. 3 vols. Glasgow, 1754–61.

Gilpin, William. *The Life of John Wyclif*. London: Wetton and Jarvis, 1821.

Godwin, Francis. *A Catalogue of the Bishops of England, since the first planting of Christian Religion in this Island, Together with a brief History of their lives and memorable actions, so neere as can be gathered out of antiquity*. London, 1615.

Grassi, Petrus Maria. *De Ortu ac Progressu Haeresum Io. Witclefi in Anglia Presbyteri Narratio Historica*. Vicentiae, 1707.

Gratius, Orthuinus. *Fasciculus rerum expetendarum ac fugiendarum*. Coloniae, 1535.

————. *Fasciculus rerum expetendarum & fugiendarum*. Ed. Edward Brown. 2 vols. London, 1690.

The Great Chronicle of London. Ed. A. H. Thomas and I. D. Thornley. London: G. W. Jones, 1938.

Gretser, Jacob. *Controversiam Roberti Bellarmini S. R. E. Cardinalis Amplissimi Defensio*. 2 vols. Ingolstadii, 1607–9.

Grosses vollstaendiges Universal Lexicon aller Wissenschaften und Kuenste. 64 vols. Leipzig and Halle, 1732–54.

Gui, Bernard. *Manuel de l'Inquisiteur*. Ed. and trans. G. Mollat. 2 vols. Paris: Champion, 1926–7.

Hanrahan, T. J. "John Wyclif's Political Activity," *Mediaeval Studies*, XX (1958), 154–66.

Hauser, Henri. *La naissance du protestantisme*. Paris: Presses Universitaires de France, 1940.

Hazard, Paul. *The European Mind*. Trans. J. Lewis May. London: Hollis Carter, 1953.

Hermant, Jean. *Histoire des hérésies, des autres erreurs qui ont troublé l'Église, & de ceux qui en ont été les Auteurs, depuis l Naissance de Jesus Christ jusquà présent*. 3rd ed., 4 vols. Rouen, 1727.

Howard, Sir Robert. *The History of the Reigns of Edward and Richard II.; with reflections, and characters of their chief ministers and favourites*. London: F. Collins, for T. Fox, 1690.

Hudson, Anne. "A Lollard Compilation and the Dissemination of Wycliffite Thought," *Journal of Theological Studies*, N.S., XXIII (1972), 65–81.

————. "A Lollard Compilation in England and Bohemia," *Journal of Theological Studies*, N.S., XXV (1974), 129–40.

Huizinga, Johan. *The Waning of the Middle Ages*. New York: Anchor-Doubleday, 1954.

Hume, David. *The History of England from the Invasion of Julius Caesar to the Accession of Henry VII.* 2 vols. London: Millar, 1762.

————. *The History of England from the Invasion of Julius Caesar to the Revolution of 1688.* 5 vols. London: Bowyer, 1806.

Hurley, Michael. "'Scriptura sola': Wyclif and his Critics," *Traditio,* XVI (1960), 275–352.

Magistri Johannis Hus Opera Omnia. Ed. Vaclav Flajšhans and Marie Komínková. 4 vols. Prague: Vilimek, 1903–27.

Magistri Johannis Hus Tractatus de Ecclesia. Ed. S. Harrison Thomson. Boulder: University of Colorado Press, 1958.

James, Thomas. *An Apologie for John Wickliffe, shewing his conformitie with the new Church of England.* Oxford, 1608.

Kaczmarek, Lech. *Tomasz Netter-Waldensis jako obronca prymatu sw. Piotra, Studium dogmatyczno-hostoryczne.* "Poznanskie Towarzystwo przyjaciol nauk: Prace Komisji Teologiczne." Vol. III, Part I; Poznan, 1947.

Kaminsky, Howard. "The University of Prague in the Hussite Revolution: The Role of the Masters," in *Universities in Politics,* ed. J. W. Baldwin and R. A. Goldthwaite. Baltimore: Johns Hopkins University Press, 1972.

————. "Wyclifism as Ideology of Revolution," *Church History,* XXXII (1963), 57–74.

King, William. *Reflections upon Mr. Varillas his History of Heresy Book I. Tome I. as far as relates to English matters; more especially those of Wicliff.* London. 1688.

Knapp, P. A. "John Wyclif as Bible Translator: The Texts for the English Sermons," *Speculum,* XLVI (1971), 713–20.

Komenský, Jan Amos. *Haggaeus redivivus.* Prague: Kalich, 1952.

————. *Historia fratrum bohemorum.* Halae, 1702.

————. *Ksaft umirajici Matky Jednoty Bratrske.* Ed. Fr. Bily. Prague: Hynek, 1912.

Larroque, Daniel de. *Nouvelles accusations contre M. Varillas, ou Remarques critiques contre une partie de son premier livre de l'Histoire de l'hérésie.* Amsterdam, 1687.

Leff, Gordon. *Heresy in the Later Middle Ages.* 2 vols. Manchester: Manchester University Press, 1967.

————. "John Wyclif: The Path to Dissent," *Proceedings of the British Academy,* LII (1966), 143–80.

————. "Wiclif and Hus: A Doctrinal Comparison," *Bulletin of the John Rylands Library,* L (1967-8), 387–410.

————. "Wyclif and the Augustinian Tradition, with Special Reference to His *De Trinitate,*" *Medievalia et Humanistica,* N.S., I (1970), 29–39.

Leland, John. *Collectanea de rebus Britannicis.* Ed. Thomas Hearne. 6 vols. Oxford, 1774.

Lewis, Ewart, ed. *Medieval Political Ideas.* 2 vols. London: Routledge and Kegan Paul, 1954.

Lewis, John. *The History of the Life and Sufferings of the Reverend and Learned John Wicliffe, D.D.* London: Knaplock and Wilkin, 1720. New ed.; Oxford: Clarendon Press, 1820.

Loserth, Johann. *Huss und Wiclif. Zur Genesis der hussitischen Lehre.* 2nd ed. rev. Munchen: R. Oldenbourg, 1925.

Titus Lucretius Carus. *On the Nature of the Universe.* Trans. R. E. Latham. Harmondsworth: Penguin, 1951.

Macaulay, T. B. *Works.* 12 vols. London: Longmans, 1898.

McFarlane, K. B. *Lancastrian Kings and Lollard Knights.* Oxford: Clarendon Press, 1972.

Maimbourg, Louis. *Histoire du grand schisme d'Occident.* 2nd ed., 2 vols. Paris, 1686.

Mallard, William. "John Wyclif and the Tradition of Biblical Authority," *Church History,* XXX (1961), 50–60.

Mason, Francis, *Vindiciae Ecclesiae Anglicanae.* 2nd ed. London, 1625.

Medicis, Sebastian. *Summa omnium haeresum et Catalogus Schismaticorum, haereticorum et idolatrarum.* Florentinae, 1581.

Milton, John. *Animadversions upon the Remonstrants Defence Against Smectymnuus.* London, 1641.

———. *Areopagitica: a speech of Mr. John Milton for the Liberty of Unlicenc'd Printing, To the Parliament of England.* London, 1644.

———. *Of Reformation Touching Church-Discipline in England: And the Causes that hitherto have hindered it.* London, 1641.

Moréri, Louis. *Le Grand Dictionnaire Historique.* Rev. ed., 10 vols. Paris, 1759.

Mudroch, Vaclav, and G. S. Couse, eds. *Essays on the Reconstruction of Medieval History.* Montreal: McGill University Press, 1974.

Mudroch, Vaclav. "John Wyclyf and Richard Flemyng, Bishop of Lincoln: Gleanings from German Sources," *Bulletin of the Institute of Historical Research,* XXXVII (1964), 239–45.

Nejedlý, Zdeněk. *Dějiny husitského zpěvu.* 2nd ed., 5 vols. Prague: Ceskoslovenska akademie ved, 1954–5.

Netter, Thomas, of Walden. *Doctrinale fidei ecclesiae catholicae contra Witclevistas et Hussitas.* 3 vols. Paris, 1532–57.

Novotny, Vaclav. *Nabozenske Hnuti Ceske Ve 14. a 15. Stoleti.* Prague: Otto, 1915.

Odlozilik, Otakar. *Wyclif and Bohemia.* Prague: Published by the author, 1937.

Palacký, František, ed. *Documenta Mag. Johannis Hus.* Prague: Tempsky, 1869.

Parker, G. H. W. *The Morning Star: Wycliffe and the Dawn of the Reformation.* Exeter: Paternoster Press, 1965.

Pecock, Reginald. *The Repressor of Over Much Blaming of the Clergy.* Ed. Churchill Babington. 2 vols. London: "Rolls Series," 1860.

Pits, John. *Relationum Historicarum de Rebus Anglicis.* Paris, 1619.

Pluquet, F. A. A. *Mémoires pour servir à l'histoire des égaremens de l'esprit humain par rapport à la religion chrétienne; ou dictionnaire des hérésies, des erreurs et des schismes; . . .* 2 vols. Paris, 1762.

Poole, R. L. "On the Intercourse between English and Bohemian Wycliffites in the Early Years of the Fifteenth Century," *English Historical Review,* VII (1892), 306–11.

Public Record Office (London) MSS.: E. 101/316/36; E. 364/8.

Ragusisio, Johannis de. *Tractatus de reductione Bohemorum.* Ed. F. Palacký. 3 vols. Wien: "Monumenta Conciliorum Generalium Seculi Decimi Quinti. Concilium Basileense," 1857–1932.

Robson, J. A. *Wyclif and the Oxford Schools.* Cambridge: Cambridge University Press, 1961.

Routley, Erik. *English Religious Dissent.* London: Cambridge University Press, 1960.

Schedel, Hartmann. *Libri Cronicarum.* Nuernberg, 1493.

Schlauch, Margaret. "A Polish Vernacular Eulogy of Wycliff," *Journal of Ecclesiastical History,* VIII (1957), 53–73.

Schmidt, Martin. "John Wyclifs Kirchenbegriff. Der Christus humilis Augustins bei Wyclif. Zugleich ein Beitrag zur Frage: Wyclif und Luther," in *Gedenkschrift für D. Werner Elert, Beiträge zur historischen und systematischen Theologie.* Ed. Friedrich Hübner with Wilhelm Maurer and Ernst Kinder. Berlin: Lutherisches Verlagshaus, 1955.

Šmahel, František. "*Doctor evangelicus super omnes evangelistas*: Wyclif's Fortune in Hussite Bohemia," *Bulletin of the Institute of Historical Research,* XLIII (1970), 16–34.

Smalley, Beryl. "The Bible and Eternity: John Wyclif's Dilemma," *Journal of the Warburg and Courtauld Institutes,* XXVII (1964), 73–89.

———. "John Wyclif's *Postilla super totam bibliam,*" *The Bodleian Library Record,* IV (1953), 186–205.

Spinka, Matthew, ed. *Advocates of Reform*. The Library of Christian Classics, XIV. London: S.C.M. Press, 1953.

———. *John Hus: A Biography*. Princeton: Princeton University Press, 1968.

———. *John Hus and the Czech Reform*. Chicago: University of Chicago Press, 1941.

———. *John Hus' Concept of the Church*. Princeton: Princeton University Press, 1964.

Stacey, John. *John Wyclif and Reform*. Philadelphia: Westminster Press, 1964.

Staehelin, Ernst, ed. *Die Verkündigung des Riches Gottes in der Kirche Jesu Christi*. 3 vols. Basel: Reinhardt, 1951–5.

Stow, John. *The Annales of England*. Ed. Howes. London, 1631.

Swiderska, H. M. "A Polish Follower of Wyclif in the Fifteenth Century," *University of Birmingham Historical Journal*, VI (1957–8), 88–92.

Tanner, Thomas. *Biblioteca Britannico-Hibernica*. London, 1748.

Tatnall, E. C. "The Condemnation of John Wyclif at the Council of Constance," *Studies in Church History*, VII (1971), 209–18.

———. "John Wyclif and *Ecclesia Anglicana*," *Journal of Ecclesiastical History*, XX (1969), 19–43.

Thomson, S. H. "Wyclif or Wyclyf?," *English Historical Review*, LIII (1938), 675–8.

Trithemius, Johannes. *Catalogus scriptorum ecclesiasticorum, sive illustrium virorum, cum appendice eorum qui nostro etiam seculo doctissimi claruere*. Coloniae, 1531.

Turrecremata, Johannes de. *Summa de ecclesia*. Venetiis, 1561.

Twysden, Roger. *An Historical Vindication of the Church of England in point of Schism, as it Stands Separated from the Roman, and was Reformed to Elizabeth*. Ed. G. E. Corrie. Cambridge: Cambridge University Press, 1847 [1657].

Urbanek, Rudolf. *Vek Podebradsky*. Prague: Laichter, 1915.

Varillas, Antoine. *Histoire des Révolutions arrivées dans l'Europe en matière de Religion*. 6 vols. Paris, 1686–8.

———. *Histoire du Wiclefianisme. Ou de la Doctrine de Wiclef, Jean Hus, et Jerom de Prague*. Lyon, 1682.

———. *Réponse de M. Varillas à la critique de M. Burnet sur les deux premiers tomes de l'Histoire des révolutions arrivées dans l'Europe en matière de religion*. Paris, 1687.

Vermaseren, B. A. "Nieuwe Studies Over Wyclif en Huss," *Tijdschrift voor geschiedenis*, LXXVI (1963), 190–212.

Vignier, Nicolas. *Recueil de l'histoire de l'Église, depuis le Baptesme de Notre Seigneur Jésus-Christ, iusques à ce temps*. Leyden, 1601.

Voltaire, F. M. A. de. *Essai sur les moeurs*. 3 vols. Paris: Garnier, 1878.

von der Hardt, Hermann, ed. *Magnum Oecumenicum Constantiense Concilium de Universali Ecclesiae Reformatione, Unione, et Fide*. 7 vols. Helmstadt: Genschius, 1696–1742.

von Schulte, Johann Friedrich. *Die Geschichte der Quellen und Literatur des Canonischen Rechts*. 3 vols. Reprint of 1875. Graz: Akademische Druck- und Verlagsanstalt, 1956.

Walsingham, Thomas. *Historia Anglicana*. Ed. H. T. Riley. 2 vols. London: "Rolls Series," 1863–4.

Wilks, M. J. "The Early Oxford Wyclif: Papalist or Nominalist?," *Studies in Church History*, V (1969), 69–98.

———. "Predestination, Property and Power: Wyclif's Theory of Dominion and Grace," *Studies in Church History*, II (1965), 220–36.

———. "*Reformatio Regni*: Wyclif and Hus as Leaders of Religious Protest Movements," *Studies in Church History*, IX (1972), 109–30.

Wilson, J. L. *John Wycliffe, Patriot and Reformer, The Morning Star of The Reformation*. New York: Funk and Wagnalls, 1884.

Wood, Anthony à. *Historia et Antiquitates universitatis Oxoniensis*. 2 vols. Oxford, 1674.

Workman, H. B. *John Wyclif*. 2 vols. Oxford: Clarendon Press, 1926.

Wray, J. J. *John Wycliffe: A Quincentenary Tribute.* London: Nisbet, 1884.
Wyclif, John. *Tractatus de Ecclesia.* Ed. J. Loserth. London: Wyclif Society, 1886.
————. *De Dominio Divino Libri Tres.* Ed. R. L. Poole. London: Wyclif Society, 1890.
Zitte, Augustin. *Lebensbeschreibung des Englischen Reformators Johannes Wiklif.* Prague, 1786.
Zopf, Johann Heinrich. *Erläuterte Grundlegung der Universal-Historie bis zum Jahr 1773.* 17th ed. rev. Halle im Magdeburgischen, 1779.

Index

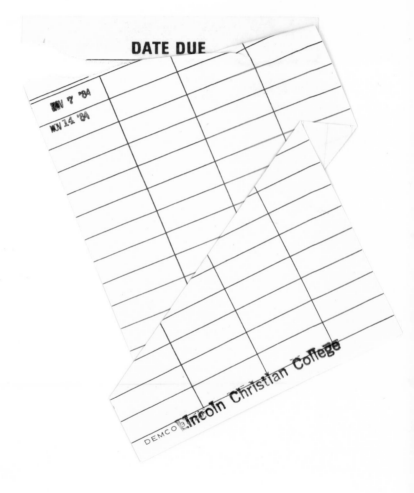